Together for Better Outcomes

ENGAGING AND INVOLVING SME TAXPAYERS AND STAKEHOLDERS

OECD
BETTER POLICIES FOR BETTER LIVES

Please cite this publication as:
OECD (2013), *Together for Better Outcomes: Engaging and Involving SME Taxpayers and Stakeholders*, OECD Publishing.
http://dx.doi.org/10.1787/9789264200838-en

ISBN 978-92-64-09651-6 (print)
ISBN 978-92-64-20083-8 (PDF)

Corrigenda to OECD publications may be found on line at: *www.oecd.org/publishing/corrigenda*.

Foreword

Revenue bodies are increasingly focused on better understanding taxpayers and taking advantage of opportunities for engaging and involving taxpayers and stakeholders where mutual or compatible interest exists. This is not least true for the large and heterogeneous SME segment, which in many countries has proven difficult and costly to administer with traditional approaches relying on enforcement and retrospective audits.

This study is intended to provide inspiration and guidance to revenue bodies wishing to further explore the potential for improving outcomes, reducing costs, improving services and generating other benefits by engaging and involving SME taxpayers and stakeholders. It provides a conceptual framework illustrating the potential benefits and situating the approach in a wider context; a comprehensive stock take of current and emerging practices; and detailed guidance to support successful design and implementation.

The study was commissioned by the Forum on Tax Administration and sponsored by the Commissioner of the Norwegian Tax Administration, Mr. Svein Kristensen. It has been prepared by a task group of SME Compliance Sub-group delegates with support from the OECD Secretariat. A total of 17 countries (Australia, Austria, Canada, Denmark, Finland, France, Hungary, Ireland, Italy, Korea, the Netherlands, New Zealand, Norway, Singapore, Switzerland, Sweden, the United Kingdom) participated in the task group. An additional three countries (Chile, Spain, Turkey) provided input to the project. The project has further benefited from input and feedback from OECD staff involved in past work on citizen participation, staff from the Danish cross-ministerial innovation platform MindLab, and staff from the Behavioural Insights Team within the UK Cabinet Office.

The Forum on Tax Administration and the SME Compliance Sub-group

The Forum on Tax Administration (FTA) was created by the Committee on Fiscal Affairs in July 2002. Since then the FTA has grown to become a unique forum on tax administration for the heads of revenue bodies and their teams from OECD and selected non-OECD countries. The work programme of the Forum is decided and overseen by a Bureau comprised of commissioners from 12 revenue bodies.

The FTA vision is to create a forum through which tax administrators can identify, discuss and influence relevant global trends and develop new ideas to enhance tax administration around the world. This vision is underpinned by the FTA's key aim which is to help revenue bodies increase the efficiency, effectiveness and fairness of tax administration and reduce the costs of compliance.

The FTA is supported by a number of specialist sub-groups and networks to help carry out its mandate: The Taxpayer Services Sub-group, the SME Compliance Sub-group, the Large Business Network, and the High Net Worth Individuals Network, and the Offshore Compliance Network.

The work of the SME Compliance Sub-group focuses on managing and improving tax compliance in the SME segment. The sub-group meets annually to provide oversight of its work programme, to review and discuss major developments, and to provide a platform for exchanging experience.

More information on the FTA, including details on products and publications, can be found at its dedicated website: *www.oecd.org/tax/fta*

The study is part of the OECD Tax Administration Information and Guidance Series, which extends across a range of areas of key interest to revenue bodies. National revenue bodies differ in a number of important ways, including in respect of their institutional legacies, the tax systems they administer, and the broader context they are part of. The series is therefore intended to inspire and inform revenue bodies rather than promote a standard approach to tax administration, which may be neither practical nor desirable.

Inquiries concerning this study should be directed to the International Co-operation and Tax Administration Division at the OECD Centre for Tax Policy and Administration.

Table of contents

Tables

Figures

Boxes

Abbreviations and acronyms

ATO – Australian Tax Office

CIT – Corporate Income Tax

CRA – Canada Revenue Agency

E&I – Engaging and Involving (or related forms, depending on context)

FTA – Forum on Tax Administration

FTE – Full Time Equivalent (measure of staff commitment)

GST – Gross Sales Tax

HMRC – Her Majesty's Revenue and Customs (United Kingdom)

HR – Human Resources

HRM – Human Resource Management

ICT – Information and Communication Technology

IR – Inland Revenue

IRAS – Inland Revenue Authority of Singapore

OECD – Organisation for Economic Co-operation and Development

PAYE – Pay As You Earn (system for withholding tax)

POS – Point of Sale

RFTS – Right From The Start (approach to compliance management)

SME – Small and Medium-sized Enterprise

SMS – Short Message Service

SMT – Social Media Technology

UK – United Kingdom

VAT – Value Added Tax

Preface

"Working Smarter" are the watchwords of modern public administration. Revenue bodies are no exception and are rightly expected to be constantly looking for opportunities to improve the way they operate and reduce costs to the public purse.

One key way that revenue bodies can meet this challenge is by working with and through others. Taxpayers' relationships with revenue bodies are frequently mediated through a range of third parties, such as tax advisers, software providers, business connections, civil society and others. These different intermediaries and the taxpayers they serve have some goals that are shared by revenue bodies. By intelligently identifying and exploiting these common interests, revenue bodies, can deliver benefits for themselves and for taxpayers; a classic win-win opportunity.

This Forum on Tax Administration publication explores how practical strategies for engaging and involving SME taxpayers and stakeholders can contribute to achieving this kind of win-win. It describes how revenue bodies can improve their understanding of compliance risks, service shortcomings and identifies possible solutions. The many examples in the report illustrate how this approach can deliver improved outcomes and a range of other benefits for taxpayers, stakeholders and society as a whole. It can also engender a virtuous circle of enhanced trust that promotes still greater levels of voluntary compliance.

Revenue bodies have a long history of involving taxpayers and stakeholders. However, this report reflects a clear trend towards doing so in more systematic, far-reaching and potentially transformative ways. This opens up a range of new opportunities and challenges. We hope that revenue bodies will find in this report useful inspiration and guidance to help them benefit from those opportunities and tackle the challenges.

I would like to thank everyone who has been involved in producing this report: the SME Compliance Sub-group, the task group, survey respondents and the OECD Secretariat. We are especially grateful to Danish innovation platform MindLab for their support throughout the process and to the Behavioural Insights Team within the UK Cabinet Office for providing valuable input and feedback.

Svein R. Kristensen

Sponsoring Commissioner

Executive summary

For many years revenue bodies have been under pressure to reduce their costs of operation, while sustaining or improving revenue collection and improving the quality of customer service for taxpayers. Internally focused efforts to improve the use of technology in revenue bodies and simplify and streamline processes have achieved a lot but, on their own, are not capable of addressing the scale of the challenge revenue bodies face, particularly in the wake of the global financial crisis. In common with many other parts of the public sector, revenue bodies are increasingly looking outside their own organisations to use the knowledge and resources of taxpayers and other stakeholders to explore win-win situations and achieve better delivery of desired outcomes.

This report, the result of a study by the Forum on Tax Administration's SME Compliance Sub-group, explores the experience to date of approaches that engage and involve SME taxpayers and stakeholders. The study was led by a task group of 17 countries and was based on a survey of revenue bodies, further research and direct engagement of the task group. Based on that work, this report:

- establishes the case for engaging and involving SME taxpayers and stakeholders;
- develops a conceptual framework establishing key concepts and situates the approach in a wider strategic context;
- presents a stock take of current and emerging practices, including considerations on key trends; and
- provides practical guidance for successful implementation.

Building on earlier work by the Sub-group and the OECD, the report offers a more in-depth understanding of what engaging and involving taxpayers and stakeholders means and the benefits it can deliver.

Across the public sector there is a growing appreciation that public services work better when designed and delivered in partnership with citizens. The report discusses how this concept of engagement & involvement (E&I) has developed and describes a spectrum of approaches, from simple communication through consultation to active collaboration, or "co-production". Chapter 2 opens with a telling example from a tax administration of the dangers of designing systems and services on the basis of assumptions about what people want and like and how engagement and involvement can diagnose and remedy the consequences. Operating in a regulatory environment does affect the scope of what can be changed through the process of engagement and involvement: a revenue body will have relatively little scope to consult about the amount of tax due. Nonetheless, engaging and involving taxpayers and stakeholders in the design of the processes for determining and paying that liability can deliver big benefits. Developments in technology are affording new opportunities for revenue bodies to engage and involve taxpayers and stakeholders and to manage the large numbers of taxpayers in the SME segment.

The report discusses the benefits that revenue bodies have found that they are able to deliver through increased engagement and involvement. These benefits are not limited to better outcomes for the revenue body in terms of improved compliance and cost reductions, significant though these are. These wider benefits include positive impacts on democratic governance and public trust, which feedback positively into attitudes towards tax compliance. Revenue bodies have also identified concrete benefits for taxpayers and stakeholders, such as lower compliance costs for SMEs, fairer competition resulting from more consistent compliance across the SME population and an improved service experience. The evidence about benefits is compelling but there is an issue around measurement. The shift in focus from outputs to outcomes, which is a general feature of modern compliance strategy and key to the assessment of engagement and involvement, poses a challenge in terms of performance management. The approach recognises the complexity of the system that it is trying to affect but it entails a much more diverse set of costs and benefits than traditional interventions based on audits. As a result, the methods of tracking those costs and benefits have to be equally sophisticated.

The review of current and emerging practices shows that a high level commitment to engaging and involving taxpayers and stakeholders is now considered central to the strategic direction and daily operations of most revenue bodies. In turn this is leading many revenue bodies to adopt a systematic approach that ensures the high level commitment is translated into changed operating practices across their operations. A number of specific examples are used to illustrate how revenue bodies have applied the approach to a wide range of their activities. It is now commonplace to involve taxpayers and stakeholders in deciding how best to provide them with information and guidance. Most revenue bodies also engage in social research, or user testing, to ensure that services are designed to meet the expectations of taxpayers and stakeholders. Many now actively collaborate with stakeholders to deliver these services. Some degree of taxpayer and stakeholder involvement in compliance risk management is quite common. Some revenue bodies have gone further and extend that involvement into the process of risk identification and prioritisation, the design of specific compliance treatments and subsequent evaluation. The types of stakeholders with which revenue bodies look to engage is widening and the report sets out a basic typology, which coupled with a list of leverage strategies can be used as a practical checklist for revenue bodies when reviewing their stakeholder engagement strategies and practices.

The chapter on implementation offers some tools and guidance for revenue bodies. The key implementation issues fall under three broad headings:

- Building capabilities and managing change: Lack of capabilities, staff resistance and risk aversion are cited as major barriers to the successful implementation of E&I approaches. Committed management, engaged staff and enabling platforms like frameworks, tools and guidance are on the other hand cited as key success factors.

- Governing E&I initiatives: The challenges of approaching SME taxpayers and stakeholders, motivating them to work together, managing expectations and driving E&I processes to a successful end were cited as another barrier.

- Demonstrating value: The lack of comprehensive metrics on which to establish the case for E&I approaches constitutes a major barrier. Performance management systems focusing on outputs are ill suited to documenting the benefits of E&I approaches, which will often be working back from the ultimate outcomes.

The chapter on implementation discusses each of these topics and concludes with a list summarising key advice for successful implementation. It also includes reference to additional resources that may be of assistance to revenue bodies.

The report finds that engagement and involvement strategies offer substantial benefits to revenue bodies themselves and substantial external benefits as well. The report concludes by encouraging revenue bodies to:

- Assess their current experience and consider opportunities for more systematic and far-reaching approaches: The collective experience with E&I approaches documented in this report is sufficiently broad and deep that there should be something to inspire everybody. Revenue bodies that already have mainstreamed E&I approaches in some areas may benefit from applying more systematic approaches or from developing more far-reaching and potentially transformative initiatives.
- Assess their current capabilities and consider opportunities for better supporting the mainstreaming of E&I approaches: E&I is increasingly recognised as a distinct approach requiring specialist capabilities not just in terms of competences, but also in terms of organisational culture, values and mind-set. This may in turn affect HRM practices (in areas like recruitment, training, remuneration and reward systems) and organisational structure. Revenue bodies may benefit from considering these issues in the context of their wider strategies and capability-building efforts.
- Assess how E&I approaches fit with their current performance evaluation framework and consider opportunities for strengthening the outcome focus: Narrow output measures are relatively easy to work with, but may channel attention and resources away from innovative approaches. Documenting outcomes and attributing them to revenue body activities (and their individual components) on the other hand presents a number of challenges. Therefore more pragmatic approaches are often required. Revenue bodies may find inspiration in previous work of the FTA.

Chapter 1

Introduction

Engaging and involving taxpayers and stakeholders offers the opportunity to mobilise knowledge and resources residing outside the revenue body. This can contribute significantly to improved outcomes, cost reductions and a range of other benefits. It can also enhance the legitimacy of the tax system and trust in the revenue body, which are crucial for voluntary compliance.

This chapter discusses the rationale of this exploratory study and sets out study objectives and content. The chapter further illustrates the methodology adopted, including details on data collection and contributing revenue bodies.

"The managers of those organisations who ignore their clients will miss potentially significant capabilities and resources." (Alford 2009: 3)

"Public services must engage and enroll citizens, families, communities, enterprises and the wider society as partners in creating better social and economic outcomes. The state, market or society alone cannot achieve this. So our goal must be a culture of participation based on the joint creation of social value." (Kippin & Lucas, 2010: 16).

Rationale for engaging and involving taxpayers and stakeholders

Revenue bodies are expected to be continuously searching for ways to do more and better with less. Increased reliance on technology, leaner organisations, and more sophisticated compliance strategies have helped respond to the pressures of rising volumes and complexity on the one hand and rising expectations on the other. The challenge has been further accentuated by the difficult budgetary climate following the 2008 global financial crisis.

Engaging and involving taxpayers and stakeholders offers the opportunity to harness knowledge and resources residing outside the revenue body. Leveraging on the knowledge, reach, credibility and efforts of others may contribute significantly to improved compliance outcomes, cost reductions, increased levels of customer satisfaction, and a range of other benefits.

By engaging and involving taxpayers and stakeholders, revenue bodies can achieve a better understanding of what the problems are, what is driving these problems, and what the appropriate solutions might be. They can also benefit from the involvement of taxpayers and stakeholders in the design, implementation or evaluation of these solutions. Engaging and involving taxpayers and stakeholders can for instance enhance the identification of risks, contribute to more tailored services and treatments, and help revenue bodies achieve greater reach through one-to-many approaches leveraged by stakeholders, technologies and media. It can also help identifying opportunities to eliminate sources of error, design more meaningful and efficient processes and solutions, or improve the functioning of the tax system in other ways.

While engaging and involving taxpayers and stakeholders offers many benefits to revenue bodies, there are also substantial external benefits involved. Engaging and involving taxpayers and stakeholders can for instance contribute to improving services, reducing the administrative costs falling on taxpayers or better promoting a level playing field. This in turn will be beneficial to society as a whole, as it creates the conditions for growth and a smooth operation of the economy. It may also be part of a virtuous circle, as enhanced trust and confidence in the revenue body and the tax system is known to also enhance voluntary compliance.

Recent work by the Forum on Tax Administration reflects how revenue bodies are increasingly recognising and taking advantage of these opportunities. The theme was first explored in the *"Right from the Start: Influencing the Compliance Environment for SMEs"* information note, which contained a number of examples of how engaging and involving taxpayers and stakeholders can contribute to enhancing the management of compliance risks for SME segment (OECD, 2012). The tendency has also been pronounced in the large businesses space increasingly characterised by "enhanced relationship" or "cooperative compliance" arrangements shifting attention from individual issues to risk management frameworks and practices more generally, and providing a platform for upfront resolution of material tax risks (OECD, 2013).

Revenue bodies are not alone in seeing the potential in working with and through others. Offering clients and stakeholders a greater role in the design and delivery of services is a major trend across the public sector in many countries. The trend is particularly prominent in health care, child care and care for the elderly, but more recently it has also spread to areas like crime prevention, maintenance of public infrastructure and monitoring of the environment. These are areas where outcomes are dependent on contributions from clients, or where input from clients and stakeholders can substitute public sector input. The literature suggests that involving clients and stakeholders in this way can lead to cost reductions, better outcomes and improved service experiences while also enhancing accountability and democratic governance (OECD, 2011a).

A number of arguments have been put forward to explain this tendency. Among the frequently cited factors are the pressure to reduce costs, increase efficiencies and improve outcomes; governments and public bodies responding to rising expectations from citizens; and the influence of the participative web (OECD 2011a). It has further been argued that public sector organisations have no choice but to engage and involve clients and stakeholders because of the nature of the challenges they are facing. This line of argument holds that many of the challenges currently faced by governments are essentially "wicked problems" (like climate change or chronic disease) that cannot be cost-effectively addressed by governments alone, but require sophisticated solutions drawing on the full range of stakeholders (Australian Public Sector Commission 2009). At a more fundamental level, it can be argued that while governments can produce outputs on their own, producing outcomes requires the participation of clients and stakeholders (Pollitt et al, 2006).

Applying these insights to tax administration would mean recognising the complexity of the compliance environment where outcomes are shaped by a range of factors not easily influenced by traditional "command and control" approaches. In this context, engaging and involving taxpayers and stakeholders offers revenue bodies with options for better understanding these factors and opens a range of options for influencing them in innovative and potentially cost-effective ways. This would seem particularly attractive for the large and heterogeneous SME segment where unintentional errors account for a significant part of the tax gap in many countries.

Engaging and involving taxpayers is, however, no quick fix or panacea. It is essentially an approach complementing existing tools or approaches, but also affecting when and how they may be applied to the best effect. As such it needs to be firmly rooted in an overall strategic approach setting the direction for the revenue body and providing orientation as to what means would seem appropriate in different circumstances. Like any other approach, it also comes with risks and challenges that need to be well considered and managed. And genuine commitment as well as a fair amount of investment in capabilities and relationships is required to lay the foundations for long-term success.

This information note provides a reference point for revenue bodies wishing to further explore this potential. The study explores how engaging and involving SME taxpayers and stakeholders can contribute to better outcomes and other benefits. Given the characteristics of the SME segment, its contribution to the tax gap and its role in the economy, and the costs and limitations of traditional approaches, the potential benefits would seem considerable.

Study objectives and content

This study has grown out of work undertaken in the Forum on Tax Administration SME Compliance Sub-group. The sub-group has explored modern compliance risk management principles and their implications with respect to designing and implementing innovative treatments, understanding and influencing taxpayer compliance behaviour, evaluating outcomes of compliance strategies and treatments, and shifting activities up in the value stream through "right from the start" measures, including early interventions and lasting changes to the compliance environment. This has led to a growing interest in the experience with engaging and involving taxpayers and stakeholders.

Against this background, the purpose of the study is to:

- establish the case for engaging and involving SME taxpayers and stakeholders;
- develop a conceptual framework establishing key concepts and situating the approach in a wider strategic context;
- present a stock take of current and emerging practices, including considerations on key trends; and
- provide practical guidance for successful implementation.

The study represents a step towards a more in-depth understanding of what engaging and involving taxpayers and stakeholders means, how it might contribute to improved outcomes and other benefits, what the wider strategic implications are, and what is required for successful implementation. The study is thus a natural extension of past work that will contribute to further bringing the various elements contained in previous studies together into a comprehensive approach to managing SME compliance and indeed to managing compliance more generally. It also represents a contribution to the growing body of literature on engaging and involving clients and stakeholders, which offers few examples from the regulatory space and few if any comprehensive sector-specific studies.

The report is structured as follows: This first chapter establishes the case for engaging and involving taxpayers and stakeholders, presents the study objectives and content, and illustrates the methodology adopted. The second chapter provides a framework for understanding the potential benefits and practical applications of the approach and applying it in a tax administration context. The third chapter offers a stock take of current and emerging practices. The fourth chapter considers some of the main challenges and success factors, and provides tools and guidance to support successful implementation. The final chapter sets out key findings and recommendations.

Methodology

The report was prepared by a task group of SME Compliance Sub-group delegates with support from the OECD Secretariat. A total of 17 countries (Australia, Austria, Canada, Denmark, Finland, France, Hungary, Ireland, Italy, Korea, the Netherlands, New Zealand, Norway, Singapore, Switzerland, Sweden, and the United Kingdom) participated in the task group.

The report is based on a survey conducted among revenue bodies to assess their practices and experience with engaging and involving taxpayers with particular focus on the SME segment; desk based research to identify key references and draw out relevant material reflecting experience, theories and conceptual frameworks; and a task group workshop to discuss concepts and methods, share experience, and work hands-on with implementation issues.

The survey was designed to capture perceived benefits; commitment expressed in high level strategic documents; frameworks, strategies and systematic practices supporting implementation; practices in a range of specific areas relevant to the management of SME compliance; and key barriers and enablers. It also included a template to identify and document examples. A total of 20 revenue bodies responded to the survey providing more than 50 closely documented examples in addition to examples and practices referred to elsewhere in the survey responses. In addition to the 17 task group countries, survey responses and examples were received from Chile, Spain and Turkey. A copy of the survey form and the related template is included as Annex 1.

The research covered academic and policy literature, the growing body of practitioner literature, and publicly available documents (for instance in the form of strategy documents, annual plans, and performance reports) reflecting revenue body practices and experience. The research phase also involved exploratory conversations with OECD staff involved with past work on citizen participation, with staff from the Danish cross-ministerial innovation platform MindLab, and with staff from the Behavioural Insights Team within the UK Cabinet Office.

The task group workshop in Oslo, hosted by the Norwegian Tax Administration and facilitated by MindLab, involved presentations, detailed discussions and hands-on collaborative work sessions. Among the issues considered were key barriers and enablers; pitfalls, challenges and success factors; implications in terms of skills, culture and organisation; and performance evaluation. The workshop was attended by 16 task group countries, the European Commission Taxation and Customs Union and OECD Secretariat staff. It included presentations by a representative of the Norwegian Association of Authorised Accountants and a video testimony by a bookkeeper in a Norwegian SME.

While the task group fully recognises the importance of the views and experiences of taxpayers and stakeholders, as an international group, it has not been practicable for it to gather their testimonies directly in any systematic way. Instead, the views and experiences of taxpayers and stakeholders are represented indirectly through the interpretations of revenue bodies or through examples including actual testimonies. The direct involvement of taxpayers and stakeholders in projects of this nature is possibly something that could be explored in future work.

Bibliography

Alford, J. (2009), *Engaging Public Sector Clients: From Service-Delivery to Co-Production*, Palgrave Macmillan and Houndmills, New York.

Australian Public Service Commission (2009), *Tackling Wicked Problems: A Public Policy Perspective*, Australian Public Service Commission, Contemporary Government Challenges, Australia.
www.apsc.gov.au/publications07/wickedproblems.htm

Kippin, H. & B. Lucas (2010), *From Big Society to Social Productivity*, 2020 Public Services Hub, RSA, United Kingdom.
http://2020psh.org/wp-content/uploads/2011/04/RSA_BigSoc_A4_04.pdf

OECD (2013), *Co-operative Compliance: A Framework: From Enhanced Relationship to Co-operative Compliance*, OECD Publishing, Paris.
DOI: *10.1787/9789264200852-en*

OECD (2012), *Right from the Start: Influencing the Compliance Environment for SMEs*, Forum on Tax Administration, OECD, Paris.
http://www.oecd.org/site/ctpfta/49428016.pdf

OECD (2011a), *Together for Better Public Services: Partnering with Citizens and Civil Society*, OECD Public Governance Reviews, OECD Publishing, Paris.
DOI: *10.1787/9789264118843-en*

Pollitt, C., G. Bouckaert & E. Loffler (2006), *Making quality Sustainable: Co-design, co-decide, co-produce, co-evaluate,* Scientific rapporteurs, 4QZ Conference.
www.vm.fi/vm/en/04_publications_and_documents/01_publications/04_public_management/20071019Making/VM_4_QC_Loppuraportti_Nettipdf.pdf

Chapter 2

The Engaging & Involving concept and its implications for tax administration

Engaging and involving citizens in the production of public services has emerged as a major trend across the public sector in many countries. The approach offers substantial benefits to governments, citizens and society as a whole, as (among other benefits) it can mobilise unused resources, contribute to better solutions and outcomes, and enhance legitimacy, trust and democratic governance.

This chapter, drawing on work by the OECD and academic literature, offers an introduction to these developments and their relevance to tax administration. The chapter relates the Engaging & Involving (E&I) concept to existing models of public participation and emerging practices of co-production. It further situates this change in perspective in the context of broader developments, notably the changing role of the public sector and the impact of new technologies. Finally the chapter lifts the perspective to elaborate on the implications for tax administrations and the management of SME compliance, including the many internal and external benefits.

Creating value for citizens with citizens

Engaging and involving taxpayers and stakeholders is the tax administration parallel to client-orientation and citizen participation in public service delivery. The approach is based on the premise that public services work better when designed and delivered in partnership with citizens in order to harness their interest, energies, expertise and ambitions (OECD, 2011a). From this perspective, citizens are not just passive recipients of public services. Instead value *for* citizens is created *with* citizens. Engaging and involving citizens is in this light a way of tapping into external resources in order to enhance the value of public services (Bason, 2010; Andersson et al, 2010).

If the knowledge and insights of citizens are not made use of, public services tend to be designed on the basis of assumptions by service providers about what citizens need and want. The experiences of service providers, however well intentioned, may be far removed from those of service users, and might not be accurate. In this context, bringing in the perspectives of taxpayers and stakeholders can prompt radical new insights, which in turn can drive innovation leading to improving outcomes or other benefits. An example from Denmark (see Box 2.1) illustrates the dramatic impact that bringing in the voices of taxpayers and stakeholders can have.

Box 2.1 Listening to user-experience in Denmark

The Danish Tax and Customs Administration has a strategic goal of achieving a "no touch" situation where individuals with simple tax affairs either will not need to interact with the revenue body or will serve themselves on the self-service interface. Surprisingly, however, the supposedly internet-savvy generation under 30 years of age seems reluctant to serve themselves and is far more likely than the average population to call the revenue body or show up at a tax centre for assistance.

To explain this situation and identify possible remedies, the revenue body cooperated with the cross-ministerial innovation unit MindLab to conduct qualitative research among a small sample of young individuals with different social and educational backgrounds. The research applied methodologies like probing, user-observation and process mapping to explore how this group interacted with the revenue body. This involved a researcher from MindLab and a project leader from the revenue body sitting in, as users tried to find information on the revenue body website or perform apparently simple operations on the self-service interface.

The research revealed that users experienced a number of barriers in serving themselves on the platform offered. Frequently these related to the structure and language of the platform being derived from paper forms never experienced by this generation of users. This led to uncertainty and even anxiety among some users. In one case, for fear of doing something wrong, a 21 year old auto mechanic named Dennis preferred to get in his car and drive for 30 minutes to the local tax office where he would wait until staff could walk him through the required actions. It turned out that part of what he needed was for somebody to translate the technical terms on the digital form to language that he could relate to.

Experiencing these situations first hand was a real eye-opener to the revenue body. With the consent of interviewees, sound bites from the research were played to the board, which went silent, as senior managers otherwise occupied with strategies and metrics suddenly connected to how some users experience apparently trivial interactions with the revenue body.

Following this aha-moment, a multi-year project team was tasked with a radical overhaul of the self-service interface. Work is still ongoing and the story about how Dennis experienced interacting with the revenue body can sometimes be heard in meeting rooms at the Danish Tax and Customs Administration.

Field observation of taxpayers is just one example of how revenue bodies can engage taxpayers to improve the understanding of their experience and the factors influencing their behaviour. This knowledge can in turn be applied to tailor products and interventions, design more meaningful processes and solutions, and improve the operation of the tax system in other ways. Revenue bodies also have a range of opportunities to explore shared or compatible interests with taxpayers and stakeholders through more direct forms of collaboration. This can provide the revenue body with leverage for compliance activities or produce other beneficial outcomes for all parties involved.

The Engaging & Involving concept

The concept of "engaging and involving" taxpayers and stakeholders captures the many ways revenue bodies may engage and involve taxpayers and stakeholders. This section will explain the concept of engaging and involving taxpayers and stakeholders – the E&I concept – and situate it in relation to some established terminologies around citizen participation. It will also discuss its meaning in relation to some emerging more extensive forms of collaboration.

Established terminologies

There is a range of established terminologies around public participation. Sherry Arnstein (Arnstein, 1969) famously introduces a "ladder" of participation ranging from non-participation (manipulation, therapy) over tokenism (information, consultation, placation) to citizen power (partnership, delegated power, citizen control). The ladder metaphor implies that it is desirable to climb up the ladder and indeed the model can be criticised for discriminating against the lower levels of engagement on the basis of arguments that should not be relevant in the context of genuine participation. This may, however, be explained by the origin of the model in the heated debates on public participation of the 1960s, and the model remains the most influential model of public participation.

The differentiating dimension on Arnstein's ladder is the degree of empowerment, i.e. the level of influence or control delegated to citizens. Another way of approaching this is looking at the information flow. Rowe and Frewer (Rowe, Frewer, 2005) distinguish between different degrees of participation using the information flow as the differentiating dimension. In their model, participation can fall into the categories of communication (with information flowing mainly from the authority to the public), consultation (with information flowing mainly from the public to the authority), and collaboration (with information flowing both ways).

Based on these terminologies and models, it is possible to establish a simple model illustrating a continuum of E&I approaches from no or limited engagement to extensive engagement.

Figure 2.1 Continuum of Engaging & Involving approaches

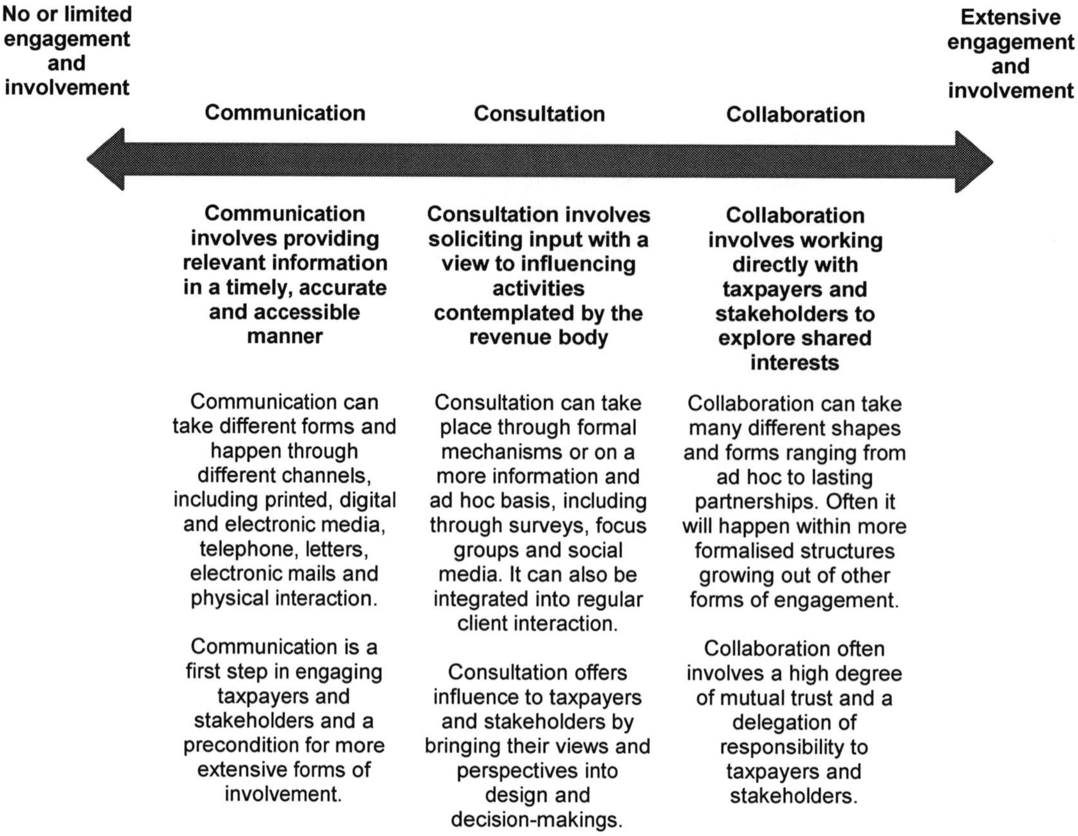

The model is useful in that it provides a framework for talking about E&I approaches. It is not intended, however, to signal a preference for some forms of E&I over others. Different levels of engagement and different methodologies will be appropriate in some contexts and circumstances and less appropriate (or even inappropriate) in others. In the words of one experienced practitioner, it is a matter of "horses for courses" (Wilcox, 1994). In this context, the model offers a shared reference and a starting point for making informed decisions about when what form of engagement are appropriate and what relationship to strive for with particular stakeholders.

In its 2011 report *"Together for better public services: partnering with citizens and civil society"*, the OECD describes different forms of participation by differentiating between the degree of intended change and the type and extent of input required. The degree of change can range from recognition of some input from users (least transformative) over the recognition of value and encouragement of contributions (intermediate) to re-location of power and control creating new structures rather than ad hoc opportunities for collaboration (transformative). The type and extent of input can vary between sporadic and distant, intermittent (or short term), and intensive and enduring (or long term).

Taken together this means that E&I approaches does not just encompasses practical challenges like with whom to interact and about what, but also more fundamental issues on how much it can and should alter the public body's current structures and the degree of influence and power delegated to citizens. Engaging and involving taxpayers and other stakeholders can therefore be more or less extensive, take many different forms, involve different parties and to different degrees, and relate to different parts of the work of the public body concerned, depending on what is deemed appropriate based on evaluation of costs and benefits as well as other considerations.

For revenue bodies, the fact that they are operating in a regulatory or compliance context (as opposed to a service context) is obviously a highly relevant factor, especially when it comes to deciding the subject matter of any specific engagement. To put it simply, a revenue body will have relatively little scope to consult about the amount of a tax liability but may benefit significantly from engaging and involving taxpayers and stakeholders in the design of the processes for determining and paying that liability.

More extensive forms of collaboration

Engagement and involvement approaches have developed over time and several forms of collaboration have emerged, including what is now known as co-creation, co-production, co-delivery and other co-concepts. Engagement and involvement in the design or setup of a solution is often referred to as co-design and engagement and involvement in the delivery or use of a solution (such as a self-service application) is often referred to as co-delivery. The government provides tools and access to information and citizens execute their own transactions. It is of course possible to co-design a system of co-delivery or just involve and engage in one of these two phases.

These concepts tend to consist of more extensive forms of engagement and involvement and thus are more collaborative. In its 2011 report the OECD uses the term co-production to describe the direct involvement of individual users and groups of citizens in the planning and delivery of public services. Co-production is "a way of planning, designing, delivering and evaluating public services which draw on direct input from citizens, service users and civil society organisations." (OECD, 2011a: 32).

The term co-production is not new (see Box 2.2). What is new is attention to it as a source of public sector innovation and reform: "Some OECD countries have recognised the innovative potential of co-production to significantly change public service delivery, and have put it forward as one element of the next phase of public service reform." (OECD, 2011a: 28).

The 2011 OECD report analysed co-production practices across a range of public service categories. The report found that co-production takes place at different stages of the policy process, from planning through delivery and evaluation. Patterns vary for different services, with most involvement in the delivery stage in personal services, and more monitoring and evaluation in general services such as environmental protection. Users are likely to be co-producers for personal services such as health and social care, and citizens input to services which are community-based. Most of the service changes could be defined as incremental, involving additions or modification of services, rather than radical transformation.

Box 2.2 Origin and development of the term co-production

The term "co-production" dates back to the 1970s. It originally related primarily to the direct involvement of citizens or clients in the public or private sectors in the production of services. It generated great interest in the 1970s and 1980s, but was not much used in subsequent years, as other models of public service reform were predominant. Co-production attracted little official interest at the start, as the concept was primarily seen as relating to volunteers, making it dependent on altruism; this did not mesh well with market principles. This emphasis also overshadowed models of co-production by clients and, thus, the potential to collaborate with users to improve services was not fully explored.

From the 1980s onwards, the models for public service improvement were predominantly managerial, with an emphasis on markets and competition, improving quality and choice, and new forms of performance management. The main policy thrust has been to improve efficiency in service delivery and enhance service quality. Part of the New Public Management approach has been to shift the organisational focus from internal processes and administrative procedures to an external focus on customers. These models of public service reform focus on professionalising delivery to customers, clients, and users to improve quality and achieve value for money.

Starting in the 1990s, commentators and practitioners highlighted the importance of citizen contributions to the public realm, alongside the more widespread market approaches.

Source: OECD (2011a), *Together for Better Public Services: Partnering with Citizens and Civil Society*, OECD Public Governance Reviews, OECD Publishing, Paris DOI: *10.1787/9789264118843-en*

Another E&I approach is the lead user method. Working with lead users has been documented to create radically novel product concepts, as lead users representing key trends in society face needs that the general market will have later. Lead users also have a high benefit from using the innovation themselves. Origins of the lead user method date back to 1986, when Eric von Hippel from Massachusetts Institute of Technology developed a structured process around searching for and integrating lead users and their ideas in production innovation. The method has recently been further developed to better support the specific innovation needs of the public sector.

Changing environment

A number of arguments have been put forward to explain the tendency to increasingly involve clients and stakeholders. This section will discuss two significant changes in the environment in which public services are delivered: the changing role of the public sector, and the opportunities offered by new technologies.

Changing role of the public sector

A growing emphasis on engaging and involving citizens is noticeable in many areas of the public sector. The role of the public sector is more and more perceived to be about delivering value for citizens and for society and less as providing services to be consumed.

Many of the challenges that the public sector faces today, such as climate changes or chronic illnesses, involve dealing with very complex problems. These problems have many and interlinked causes and no clear cut solutions. As a result there tend to be disagreements about the causes of the problems and the best way to tackle them. The problems therefore go beyond the capacity of any one organisation to understand and respond to. These complex policy challenges are sometimes referred to as "wicked problems" (Australian Public Service Commission, 2007).

Complex problems such as these cannot be solved by simple central planning. When solutions are more likely to be controversial and may, for instance, demand a potential radical change in lifestyle of citizens, they are difficult to solve in a top-down manner. As a result, they will require the consent, and often the active participation, of citizens (Andersson et al 2010).

As public sector problems are becoming more complex and interlinked, the view on what the public sector should deliver is changing. There is a shift from seeing citizens as dependents on public services to a government-citizen relationship of co-dependency and collaboration (Andersson et al, 2010; Bason, 2010). Shifting the focus from outputs to outcomes is at the core of this development, which emphasises the role of citizen support for increased quality (OECD, 2011a). Outputs are the number and quality of services provided, while outcome is the desired impact that is achieved.

The shift toward outcomes puts focus on the capability of the public sector to deliver value for citizens and not just provide services to be consumed (Coats & Passmore, 2008). In practice, this way of thinking acknowledges that citizens do not want more hospitals or more police officers; they want to be healthy and safe. By contrast, standard approaches which are focused primarily on outputs will make it difficult to focus on causes rather than symptoms.

The challenge for the public sector is to deliver more value to citizens with fewer resources. It is therefore necessary to focus on outcomes, while recognising the need to reduce costs. A high level of effectiveness means that a good outcome is achieved with a minimum of resources. Cost cutting strategies that rely on appearing to succeed by meeting output targets with fewer resources, while degrading actual outcomes, are increasingly challenged as both disingenuous and ineffective: "The current model for public service reform focuses attention on easily costed and easily delivered changes, siphoning attention and money away from preventative interventions, which are often difficult to model." (Boyle & Harris, 2009: 9).

How the public sector delivers also needs to correspond with citizens' expectations. Dealings with the public sector have to provide a positive experience, and fit democratic traditions (Bason, 2010). The emergence of engaging and involving approaches needs to be understood in this context which also helps to improve understanding of the benefits of such approaches. For public bodies concerned with issues of compliance, the delivery of positive experiences helps engender a relationship of trust between the citizen and the regulator and trust directly affects the degree of voluntary compliance that is observed.

Opportunities offered by new technologies

These changes in the perceived role and expectations of the public sector are taking place at a time when more and more people have access to technology. New technologies create additional demands for transparency and speed of response by public bodies, but it also provides opportunities for resolving the tension between rising expectations and fixed or falling resources.

The example in Box 2.3 illustrates how new technologies can be used to obtain direct feedback from users of public services on a systematic basis. The example relates to street maintenance, but similar examples can be found in park up-keep and environmental protection (OECD, 2011a). In these and other areas, citizen input can alert authorities to risks and issues, which can in turn facilitate the work and reduce the costs of public bodies. At the same time, such platforms may contribute to increased awareness among citizens of public goods and lead to citizens mobilising their resources to prevent or solve problems that otherwise would have had to be fixed by public bodies.

At the same time new technologies offer opportunities for increased reliance on self-service solutions, automated processes for data exchange and consolidation, and technology-leveraged monitoring of critical functions and processes. For instance in health, the well-being (and ultimately life-expectancy) of patients with chronic diseases can be enhanced by equipment monitoring critical health indicators and exchanging data with authorities. Similarly in tax administration, new technologies (for instance forms of performing and recording transactions) have important implications for how tax compliance can be supported and monitored, which opens up exciting new territory for collaboration with taxpayers and stakeholders.

Box 2.3 Open source street maintenance

Fix My Street is a combined website and smart-phone application to help people report, view, or discuss local problems they have found to their local authorities by simply locating them on a map. It was launched in the United Kingdom in early February 2007.

Among the problems reported are abandoned vehicles; dog fouling, fly tipping and litter; fly posting and graffiti; poor or missing lightning; and potholes or other unsafe road conditions. Identified problems are reported to the relevant local council. Users can debate particular problems on the website thereby in effect lobbying for authorities to resolve them or potentially identifying alternative community-driven solutions.

As of early March 2013, almost 2 500 problems had been reported by users in the past week, and more than 5 000 problems were reported to have been fixed in the past month, which implies that the observations have been highly relevant to authorities.

The site is the project of a charity that has grown out of a community of volunteers. It was originally financed by a government innovation fund. It is now funded by commercial work and donations. The source code is available under the GNU reciprocity-based open source license. It has been used for *FiksGataMi* in Norway and similar sites in New Zealand and California.

Source: Based on information available on *www.fixmystreet.com* as of early March 2013

Implications for tax administration

The general trends in the public sector just described have also affected the task of tax administration. Consequently we have seen a steady development of the compliance strategies used by revenue bodies over recent years that mirrors those trends. This has included an increasing focus on engaging and involving taxpayers and other stakeholders to deliver improved outcomes at lower costs. Revenue bodies have also been making good use of the opportunities afforded by new technology. This progression has been reflected in, and to some extent foreshadowed by, the work of the OECD and the Forum on Tax Administration. A brief overview of some of the FTA's more recent work shows how tax compliance strategies have developed along these lines.

Risk management focus leads to a broader perspective…

Traditionally, many revenue bodies utilized a strategy based on deterrence through the use of audits and fines. Gradually a more holistic view has emerged with more multi-faceted approaches and a focus on understanding risks. The FTA report *"Compliance Risk Management: Managing and Improving Tax Compliance"* from 2004 described how a risk management framework could help revenue bodies to prioritise risks and choose appropriate treatments – see Figure 2.2. At the heart of that framework is the analysis of the underlying drivers of taxpayer behaviour. Effective treatment strategies can only be identified once those drivers are properly understood. In principle, E&I approaches can be applied in all phases of this compliance risk management framework.

Figure 2.2 Compliance risk management framework

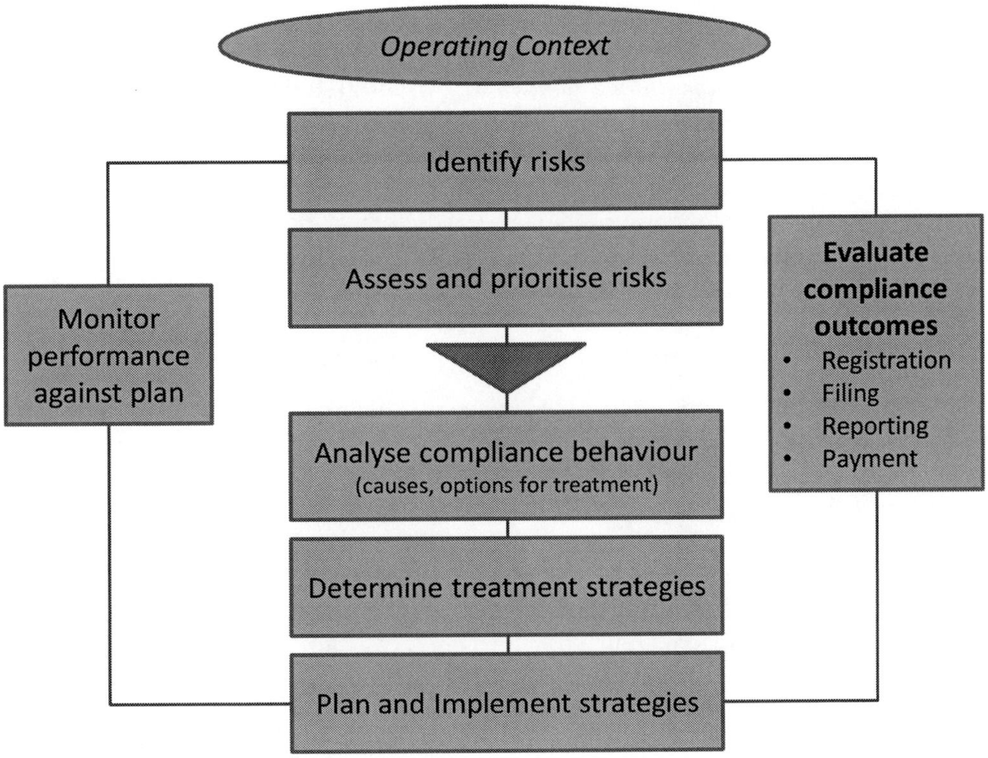

Source: OECD (2004), *Compliance risk management: managing and improving tax compliance,* Forum on Tax Administration, OECD, Paris.

The FTA note *"Managing and Improving Compliance: Recent Developments in Compliance Risk Treatments"* from 2009 discusses compliance interventions that are more and more tailored to address specific risks and that often consist of a package of several different treatments, e.g. education and communication, as well as enforcement.

The central importance that understanding taxpayer behaviour now plays in modern risk management naturally drives revenue bodies towards increasing the engagement and involvement of taxpayers. This recognises that taxpayers are not a homogeneous group and that effective interventions are responsive to the diversity of their attitudes to tax compliance and the underlying reasons for those attitudes. Armed with the understanding that engagement and involvement provides, revenue bodies are better equipped to design treatments that are more effective and long-lasting. This is as true of taxpayers exhibiting a desire not to comply, as it is of those who are willing to do the right thing.

...and a stronger focus on effectiveness

The focus on risk management also puts focus on the need to measure the effects, or outcomes, of different interventions. The result cannot only be judged by measuring outputs such as the number of audits or educational activities. The FTA note *"Evaluating the Effectiveness of Compliance Risk Treatment Strategies"* from 2010 recognised that most countries had started to develop methods and/or frameworks for measuring effectiveness but acknowledged that further development was needed.

A compliance strategy relying on diverse treatments not only requires the means to measure the effectiveness; it also requires a capability to choose the right form of treatment in the right circumstances. As explained, doing so depends on being able to understand what drives taxpayer behaviour. The FTA note *"Understanding and Influencing Taxpayers' Compliance Behaviour"* from 2010 describes the most important drivers of individual taxpayers compliance behaviour. These were grouped into five categories (economy, norms, deterrence, opportunity and fairness) and discussed on the basis of revenue body experience and academic literature. The note acknowledges the limitations of standard economic models as predictors of behaviour. It also emphasises that the five categories of drivers should not be looked at in isolation, as in practice they interact in complex ways to generate sometimes unpredictable outcomes.

... which highlights the need for cooperative approaches

Involving taxpayers and engaging them in dialogue is strongly linked to the perception of procedural fairness of the treatment of the revenue body. The FTA note *"Right from the Start: Influencing the Compliance Environment for Small and Medium-sized Enterprises"* from 2012 put the risk management approach and the acquired knowledge together into a holistic approach with the purpose of creating situations in which compliance is achieved right from the start. It gives a practical framework for revenue bodies to generate value (to themselves, taxpayers and society) by exploring systematic and coherent strategies to create an environment that influences compliance processes and behaviours before the actual reporting takes place. The note asserts that in order to achieve this, it is of particular importance to involve and engage taxpayers and other stakeholders. The holistic approach is nicely summarised by figure 2.3, taken from the report.

The context or compliance environment is important for the behaviour of the taxpayer and the revenue body is part of this context. Compliance or non-compliance with tax rules is the outcome of an ongoing interaction between government, revenue bodies and taxpayers. Compliance management has to take these different actors into account. Revenue bodies should not only focus on taxpayers but also on what they do themselves and how they perform, because that performance is itself a driver of taxpayer behaviour. The aim is to create and support an environment that is conducive to compliance by engaging and involving taxpayers.

In its most recent work the FTA has highlighted that revenue bodies are increasingly looking to work with taxpayers to find ways in which tax compliance can be built into the systems they use to administer their businesses and interact with the revenue body. This type of approach reduces the need for costly after the fact interventions to correct errors. This not only delivers savings for the revenue body but also reduces the costs of compliance for businesses, and those costs are particularly significant in the SME sector. This illustrates how the process of engagement and involvement directly supports the delivery of better outcomes and effectiveness, rather than the more limited goal of improved efficiency.

Figure 2.3 Dimensions of "right from the start" approach

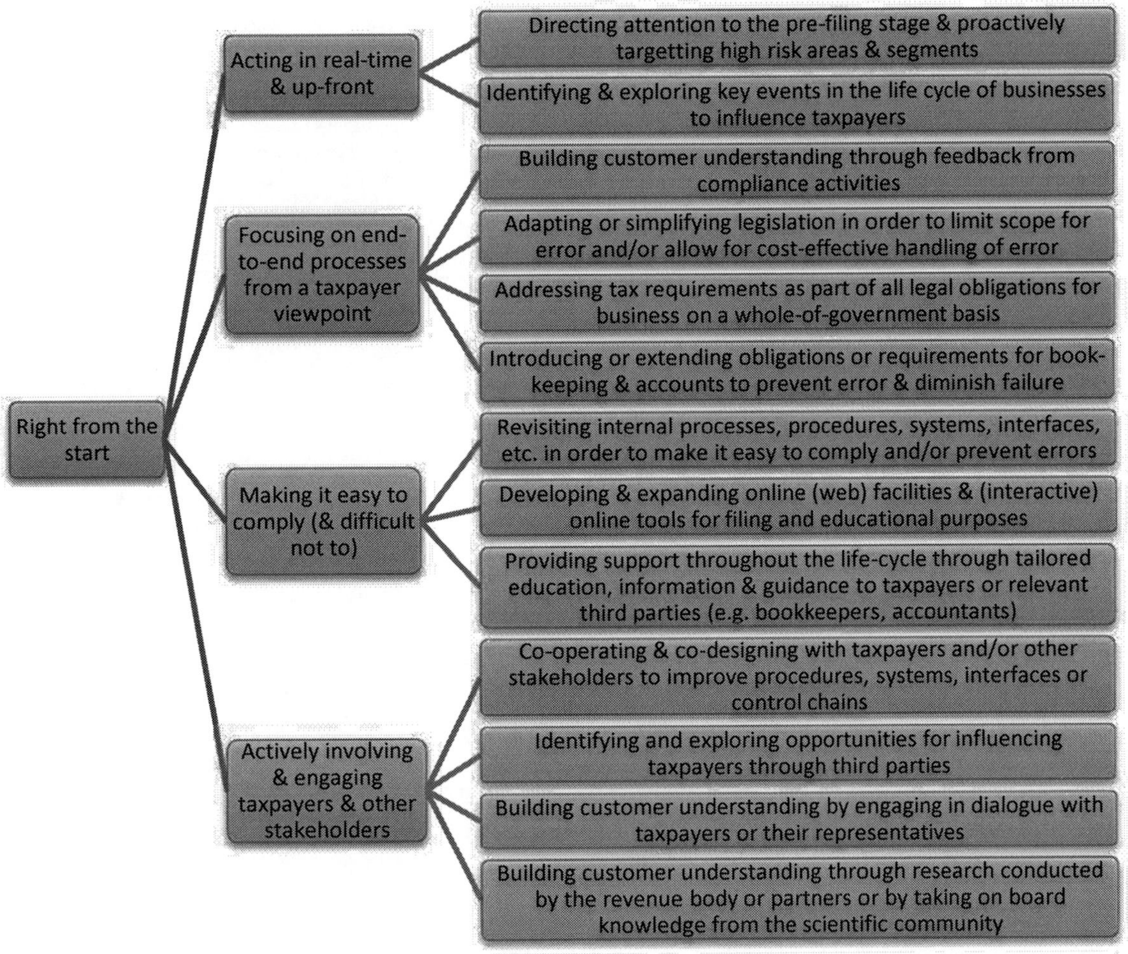

Source: OECD (2012), *Right from the Start: Influencing the Compliance Environment for SMEs*, Forum on Tax Administration, OECD, Paris.

Benefits of Engaging & Involving approaches

Engaging and involving can bring benefits to the revenue body, taxpayers, stakeholders, and society as a whole. This section, drawing on literature and survey responses, will elaborate in more detail on these benefits. The section also briefly touches upon the costs of E&I approaches, and the challenge of documenting benefits and establishing business cases, which is discussed in more detail in Chapter 4.

Benefits identified in the literature

Literature and research point to the many benefits that can be achieved by engaging and involving citizens. The 2011 OECD report outlines the benefits of more extensive forms of involvement (see Box 2.4) and points out that early experience suggest that co-production lead to cost reductions, better service quality and improved user satisfaction (OECD 2011a).

Box 2.4 The case for co-production

Co-production can help make better use of resources and contain service costs: Co-production offer a new approach to deliver more (or the same) with less by tapping into individual resources and reducing the need for expensive services. It can help to increase service effectiveness, tackle service failures, and identify solutions to complex problems

Co-production can help identify solutions to complex problems and contribute to enhancing societal and individual well-being: The size and nature of the challenges facing governments is prompting recognition that governments cannot tackle the major challenges of the 21st century alone. Global problems – such as climate change and water shortages – and lifestyle and health problems – such as obesity, chronic health conditions and other disorders leading to social exclusion (e.g. depression) – strain government resources. Delivery of traditional services, however effective, will not address these problems. Solutions require behavioural changes from both service professionals and users, and the mobilisation of community efforts.

Co-production can complement and strengthen existing reform approaches and instruments for change: The current emphasis on partnering with citizens as a potential tool in the continued transformation of public services is partly the result of reaching a leveling-out of the impacts of other models, such as efficiency improvements through competition and partnerships with the private sector. Approaches based on partnerships with citizens can, however, be complementary to and/or support other approaches to service improvement (e.g. the use of new technologies in government).

Co-production can improve democratic governance and build public trust: Citizen involvement in service delivery also reflects a broader democratic and active citizenship agenda developed over the past 20 years. Governments across OECD countries have been working to fight growing democracy deficits and to work more closely with their citizens. This has involved a range of approaches and activities: from giving information to consultation to participation. While distinct from public engagement, co-production has the potential to further the public engagement agenda.

Co-production can strengthen communities and build social capital: Co-production strengthens social capital through community involvement and civic participation. It also enhances trust and shared values, which are the basis for active citizenship.

Source: OECD (2011a), *Together for Better Public Services: Partnering with Citizens and Civil Society*, OECD Public Governance Reviews, OECD Publishing, Paris DOI: 10.1787/9789264118843-en

It is thus well established that E&I approaches can contribute to improved outcomes, cost reductions and a range of other benefits. Part of the value proposition lies in creating value with, rather than for, clients and users (Bason, 2010). At the same time costs are reduced by leveraging on the knowledge and resources of clients and users and by preventing problems rather than fixing them at a later stage (Boyle, et al 2010; Bason, 2010).

Research has also documented that knowledge residing outside public organisations is critical to innovation. Von Hippel has examined the possible contribution to innovation by lead users and has shown that these can often contribute more to innovation than producers (Von Hippel, 2010). Bason similarly points out: "Even though citizens may often be very motivated to contribute their time and expertise, and indeed experience that their participation is meaningful and empowering, that is not the main point. The point is that public sector organisations desperately need citizens' participation to better understand what they experience, how their experience could be improved and their behaviour might be changed." (Bason, 2010: 153-54).

The benefit for revenue bodies lies not just in cost reductions and improved outcomes. E&I approaches contribute to building trust and legitimacy not just among taxpayers and stakeholders directly involved, but also more generally. This is well documented in the behavioural and regulatory sciences literature. Valerie Braithwaite for instance establishes that: "authorities develop trust and build their legitimacy, not through giving people the outcomes they want, which is often impossible, but rather through observing their right to a fair hearing and respectful treatment." (Braithwaite, 2008).

Studies also show that the perception of procedural fairness is linked both to the acceptance of a specific decision and to the inclination to comply with laws and rules more generally (Tyler, 2001).

Benefits identified by revenue bodies

Survey responses and workshop discussions demonstrate that the benefits perceived by revenue bodies in large part are identical to the picture established through the literature review – see Table 2.1 for some illustrative quotes from the survey responses. Revenue bodies generally identified improved compliance outcomes, cost reductions, and improved service experiences as the key benefits of E&I approaches from a revenue body perspective. A number of revenue bodies further pointed to the benefits in terms of enhanced legitimacy and trust.

Table 2.1 Perceived benefits by revenue bodies

Australia	A huge advantage of early engagement is the return on investment provided by appropriate use of users or the community. When users are involved early in the design of products, tools or law changes that affect them, it means issues or possible obstacles to compliance can be identified early. Design modifications can also be made whilst the design is still in draft consequently there are fewer modifications at a point further down the design process, where it becomes more costly to rectify. Fixes and changes made before a design is actually implemented (but still in prototype form) save the organisation time, money and impact greatly on perceptions of professionalism and integrity (i.e. spending of public money).
Canada	The engagement of taxpayers and stakeholders serves to provide revenue bodies with an understanding of the taxpayers' viewpoint, which can in turn be used to refine and develop programs in order to improve the overall level of voluntary compliance. In addition, feedback from taxpayers and stakeholders can be used to improve risk assessment models that are used to identify instances of non-compliance.
Denmark	The benefits of E&I to the Danish Tax and Customs Administration are improved compliance, increased efficiency and an improved foundation for initiatives which will also lead to a higher level of acceptance and understanding among the taxpayers. If we know our target groups' behaviour and needs better, we can design treatments with a stronger impact. We can also save resources through co-production, where taxpayers or stakeholders with better access to target groups actively engage in delivering services in co-operation with the tax administration.
Singapore	The information arising from the engagement helps to shape the design of policies, strategies and programmes, and to ensure the feasibility of the programmes that IRAS intends to roll out. It also enhances the buy-in of taxpayers towards the programmes.

Source: Illustrative quotes from the survey responses

Approaching the benefits identified at the level below the high level outcomes, the benefits can generally be explained by three (mutually reinforcing) factors:

- **Improved understanding of taxpayers and stakeholders:** By engaging and involving taxpayers and stakeholders, revenue bodies can improve their understanding of what factors are causing compliance risks or affecting the service experience. They can also improve their understanding of the environment in which taxpayers and stakeholders are operating. This can in turn inform strategies, activities and products.
- **Leverage from stakeholders:** By engaging and involving stakeholders, revenue bodies can achieve greater reach, explore synergies and avoid duplication of efforts. Stakeholders like SME industry bodies and intermediaries often have shared (or at least compatible) interests with revenue bodies and may be better positioned to influence SME taxpayers. They may also be able to influence factors in the compliance environment, including how technologies are applied to support the process from transaction to filing and payment.
- **Enhanced trust and legitimacy:** By engaging and involving stakeholders, revenue bodies can enhance trust and legitimacy, which are key factors driving voluntary compliance. This can in turn be part of a virtuous circle, as enhanced trust and legitimacy can also facilitate further engagement.

The benefits of E&I approaches, however, are not limited to revenue bodies. Survey responses and workshop discussions also pointed to the numerous benefits for taxpayers and stakeholders. These generally fall in four categories:

- **Reduced administrative burden:** Reducing the administrative burden and compliance costs is a top priority for SME taxpayers and SME representative bodies. Working with the revenue body offers them the opportunity to identify key problem areas and contribute to solutions.
- **Fair competition:** Compliant SME taxpayers and SME representative bodies have a shared interest with the revenue body in addressing unfair competition and promoting a level playing field.
- **Improved service experience:** The input of taxpayers and stakeholders can contribute to strengthening the customer perspective and improving the service experience. This may involve services more tailored to customer needs and more differentiated approaches, including faster and smoother processes for low-risk taxpayers.
- **Business opportunities:** For some stakeholders, for instance intermediaries, working with the revenue body can make good business sense, as they may see opportunities to promote or develop their services and products.

This means that there is a range of shared or compatible interests that revenue bodies can explore to create win-win situations motivating the contributions of taxpayers and stakeholders. A number of other incentives were also pointed out. These include the opportunity to contribute to safeguarding and developing a public asset or, in the words of some revenue bodies, the opportunity to contribute to national development. These benefits relate to how taxpayers and stakeholders identify with the high-level purposes of the tax system and the revenue body. This identification is naturally an important factor (beyond self-interest and any material compensation offered) motivating taxpayers and stakeholders to contribute.

Demonstrating benefits

The discussion of potential benefits demonstrates that they are quite diverse. To make informed choices about when E&I approaches are preferable to alternative approaches, revenue bodies need a framework within which to assess costs and benefits. The issue of measurement is considered from a practical point of view and in more detail later in this report, but it is worth concluding this chapter with a few general remarks on the subject.

Shifting the focus of compliance strategy from outputs to outcomes does pose a challenge in terms of performance management. Traditional strategies focused on the detection and correction of error and were, relatively, simple to track in terms of costs and benefits. For one thing, almost all of the measures used could be internal to the revenue body (its costs, its yield). Strategies that emphasise error prevention and greater collaboration are inherently more complex to measure. This issue is not confined to the SME sector either. The report published alongside this one on the topic of co-operative compliance in the large business sector has to confront the same question.

The diversity of the potential benefits, and costs, also suggests that a mix of measures will be necessary to obtain a good overview of how well a compliance strategy that embraces engagement and involvement is performing in terms of outcomes. That mix of measures is likely to include both quantitative and qualitative elements.

Bibliography

Alford, J. (2009), *Engaging Public Sector Clients: From Service-Delivery to Co-Production*, Palgrave Macmillan and Houndmills, New York.

Andersson, E., S. Burall & E. Fenell (2010), *Talking for a change: a distributed dialogue approach to complex issues,* Involve, London. *www.involve.org.uk/wp-content/uploads/2011/03/Involve2010TalkingforaChange2.pdf*

Arnstein, S.R. (1969), "A Ladder of Citizen Participation." *Journal of the American Institute of Planners*, Vol. 35, pp 216-224.

Australian Public Service Commission (2009), *Tackling Wicked Problems: A Public Policy Perspective*, Australian Public Service Commission, Contemporary Government Challenges, Australia. *www.apsc.gov.au/publications07/wickedproblems.htm*

Bason, Christian (2010), *Leading Public Sector Innovation: Co-creating for a Better Society*, Policy Press, Bristol.

Boyle, D. & M. Harris (2009), *The challenge of co-production: How equal partnerships between professionals and the public are crucial to improving public services*, Nesta, London. *www.nesta.org.uk/library/documents/Co-production-report.pdf*

Braithwaite, V. (2008), "Tax Evasion" in M. Tonry (ed.), *Handbook on Crime and Public Policy*, Oxford University Press, Oxford.

Coats, D. & E. Passmore (2008), *Public Value: The Next Steps in Public Service Reform*, Work Foundation, London. *www.theworkfoundation.com/assets/docs/publications/201_PV_public_service_reform_final.pdf*

OECD (2004), *Compliance Risk Management: Managing and Improving Tax Compliance,* Forum on Tax Administration, OECD, Paris. *www.oecd.org/tax/taxadministration/33818656.pdf*

OECD (2009), *Managing and Improving Compliance: recent Developments in Compliance Risk Treatments*, Forum on Tax Administration, OECD, Paris. *www.oecd.org/tax/taxadministration/42490764.pdf*

OECD (2010a), *Understanding and Influencing Taxpayer's Compliance Behaviour,* Forum on Tax Administration, OECD, Paris. *www.oecd.org/dataoecd/58/38/46274793.pdf*

OECD (2010b), *Evaluating the Effectiveness of Compliance Risk Treatment Strategies*, Forum on Tax Administration, OECD, Paris. *www.oecd.org/document/31/0,3746,en_2649_33749_46282143_1_1_1_1,00.html*

OECD (2011a), *Together for Better Public Services: Partnering with Citizens and Civil Society*, OECD Public Governance Reviews, OECD Publishing, Paris. DOI: *10.1787/9789264118843-en*

OECD (2012), *Right from the Start: Influencing the Compliance Environment for SMEs,* Forum on Tax Administration, OECD, Paris. *www.oecd.org/dataoecd/41/14/49428016.pdf*

Rowe, G. & L. J. Frewer (2005), "A Typology of Public Engagement Mechanisms", *Science, Technology, & Human Values*, Vol. 30, Issue 2, Spring 2005, pp.251-290. *www.sparc.bc.ca/index.php?option=com_rubberdoc&view=doc&id=371:a-typology-of-public-engagement-mechanisms&format=raw&type=pdf*

Tyler, T. R. (2001), *Trust and law-abidingness: a proactive model of social regulation*, Centre of Tax System Integrity, The Australian National University, Canberra. *http://regnet.anu.edu.au/sites/default/files/CTSI-WorkingPaper16-full.pdf*

Von Hippel, E. (2010), "The role of lead users in innovation", pp. 411-428 in B. H. Halland and N. Rosenberg: *Handbook of the Economics of Innovation*, Vol. I, Academic Press, Burlington.

Wilcox, D. (1994), *The Guide to Effective Participation*, open source participation guide. *www.partnerships.org.uk/guide/index.htm*

Chapter 3

Current and emerging practices

Revenue bodies engage and involve taxpayers and stakeholders in many ways. This is not least true for the SME segment where engaging and involving taxpayers and stakeholders has emerged as an important source of knowledge and leverage – contributing significantly to improved compliance outcomes, better services, and enhanced legitimacy and trust.

This chapter, drawing on survey responses and examples provided by revenue bodies, provides a comprehensive stock take of current and emerging practices. It starts with high-level commitment and frameworks before proceeding to go over formal consultation mechanisms and then practices in the key areas of information and guidance, compliance risk management, and systemic solutions. Particular attention is paid to systematic and innovative approaches, as well as approaches where benefits have been documented or a plausible business case has been developed.

The chapter concludes with reflections on the overall picture emerging, including a synthesis of stakeholders involved and leverage strategies applied, which may have value as a diagnostic tool and a source of inspiration.

Commitment and frameworks

A natural starting point for a stock take of current and emerging practices is the commitment expressed to engaging and involving taxpayers and stakeholders. The survey instrument contained a set of questions to this effect. These questions addressed how intentions to engage and involve taxpayers and stakeholders were reflected in high level strategy documents, planning documents and performance accounts, and other external communication.

This section discusses the commitment expressed to engaging and involving taxpayers and stakeholders before proceeding to discuss how frameworks, methodologies and toolkits may support the translation of this commitment into changed practices.

High-level commitment

It is clear from the responses that engaging and involving taxpayers and stakeholders is considered central to the strategic direction and daily operations of most revenue bodies. There is a strong recognition that the approach is central to making better use of resources through leveraging on the knowledge, reach, credibility and efforts of others. It is also well understood that it can contribute to other benefits by reducing compliance costs, maintaining a level playing field, safeguarding the legitimacy of the tax system and improving its operation, and driving voluntary compliance.

This commitment is in some cases prominently reflected in high-level strategy documents – see Table 3.1 for some illustrative examples.

The importance of Engaging & Involving (E&I) approaches as a key enabler is also reflected in planning documents and performance accounts. Revenue bodies increasingly publish annual or multi-year planning documents, and it is common for these to underscore commitment to E&I approaches (as in the Finnish example above) or include reference to specific strategies and activities involving an E&I component. Annual reports intended for the public are also likely to highlight E&I activities reflecting positively on the revenue body.

Other external communication also reflects increasing focus on E&I activities. This is true for communication directed at taxpayers and stakeholders with whom the revenue body is seeking to establish a closer relationship as well as for communication directed at the wider public. Such communication may serve to reassert commitment, provide leverage for actual activities, and to harvest wider reputation benefits.

Table 3.1 Commitment to Engaging & Involving approaches

Australia	The *Strategic Statement 2010-15* emphasises that the revenue body should work with the community to make the tax and superannuation systems shared assets. "Being consultative, collaborative and willing to co-design" is one of six values underpinning the strategic statement. The *2012-13 Corporate Overview* underscores the commitment to "co-designing user-based changes to administrative processes, products and services".
Canada	The CRA's *Annual Report to Parliament* outlines the high level commitment to engage and involve taxpayers and stakeholders: "Our strategic goal is to make compliance easier for taxpayers and their representatives by providing them with the information and services they need to voluntarily comply with tax laws." The strategic "Vision 2020" document foresees an expanded role of this commitment: "Integrating the taxpayer experience will require the Agency to stand in the shoes of a taxpayer, tax intermediaries or benefit recipient to better anticipate and respond to their service needs. By integrating the experience for taxpayers, benefit recipients, and tax intermediaries, we can make compliance easier and reduce the red tape burden, which helps the Canadian economy."
Finland	The Finnish Tax Administration's *Annual report 2011* emphasises the commitment to engaging and involving taxpayers and stakeholders: "The Finnish Tax Administration has extensive co-operation with the public administration and other authorities, the private sector and organisations representing its customers' interests. The purpose of co-operation with Finnish stakeholders is to promote the exchange and collection of information and make the conduct of tax business easier through improved service and guidance. By cooperating with its stakeholders, the Finnish Tax Administration also wants to make tax control more effective, to ensure smooth payment operations and to provide tax recipients with more accurate tax revenue forecasts."
New Zealand	The high-level vision for New Zealand Inland Revenue set out in the *IR for the Future* strategy document is: "We work with customers and other organisations to make compliance easy and to give New Zealanders confidence that everyone pays and receives the right amount." The document further identifies "We improve the efficiency and effectiveness of government through working with other agencies and private providers" as one of six priorities for the organisation, and clarifies that this includes seeking opportunities to work with external parties, understanding businesses and working with them to achieve mutual benefits, co-designing services with others, and managing relationships based on the needs of the situation. This ambition is underpinned by the cultural value of "Working together: We work together and with other organisations to deliver better services and value".

Sources: Australian Taxation Office : *www.ato.gov.au/About-ATO/About-us/In-detail/Key-documents/Strategic-statement-2010-15/*; Canada Revenue Agency: *www.cra-arc.gc.ca/gncy/nnnl/2011-2012/menu-eng.html;* Finnish Tax Administration: *www.vero.fi/download/noname/%7BA0CC02D3-58DE-480E-9297-6CFCE1F578A9%7D/7514*; Inland Revenue: *www.ird.govt.nz/aboutir/reports/business-plan/irftf-2011/*

Embedding Engaging & Involving approaches

Survey responses and examples also provided some insights into how some revenue bodies are adopting more systematic approaches to support the translation of the commitment into changed practices across their business. This includes comprehensive frameworks situating E&I approaches in the broader strategic and organisational context, as well as more practical guidance in the form of methodologies and toolkits.

Two revenue bodies (Australia and Singapore) reported that they are developing frameworks to support E&I activities. The frameworks, which are known as "Effective Engagement Framework" and "Stakeholder Engagement Framework" respectively, have come about as result of extensive internal consultation and are still being adjusted to reflect this. The frameworks therefore cannot be referenced in detail, although they are at an advanced stage of development and are likely to soon be available. Yet it is helpful to highlight some high-level features:

- **Explicit commitment:** The frameworks reaffirm commitment to engaging and involving taxpayers and stakeholders, set out the value proposition, and connect to broader strategies and objectives;
- **Guiding principles and values:** The frameworks clarify key concepts, set out guiding principles and values to support consistent practices across different business areas, and emphasise the importance of maintaining a holistic perspective;
- **Focus on barriers and enablers:** The frameworks identify key barriers and enablers, address the need to integrate the approach in larger capability building and change management efforts, and recognises that success is to a large extent dependent upon staff mind-set, values and culture; and
- **Link to performance evaluation:** The frameworks explore the link to performance evaluation, and emphasise the importance of establishing reliable outcome measures as well as measures for the effectiveness of the engagement itself.

The ATO "Effective Engagement Framework" promotes a user-centric design methodology known as Integrated Administrative Design. This methodology is based on three principles: to place the end-users at the centre of the design process; to ensure that all stakeholders share an understanding of the intent and scope of the change; and to design the whole change end-to-end before embarking on detailed design of individual components and products. These principles would seem consistent with some of the recommendations set out in the co-production literature.

It is increasingly common to set up units dedicated to user-testing or user-centric design. The revenue bodies in Australia, the Netherlands and Norway all have mature user-testing facilities in place where products and processes can be tested with users before the actual implementation. By involving taxpayers and stakeholders at this early stage, their input and feedback can be fed into the design process to ensure that the final product better meet their needs and expectations. The Norwegian experience is described in Box 3.1.

Box 3.1 Collaborative usability testing in Norway

Realising potential savings from co-production in the form of self-service and self-reporting requires a high degree of user-friendliness in the online tools offered to SMEs. To this end, the Norwegian Tax Administration established an internal usability lab in 2010.

While both testers and observers contribute to the list of findings from each test, some of the most significant changes come about when observers have the opportunity to see revenue body proposals from the SME taxpayers' viewpoints.

In 2012, for example, early tests of an information service for tax withholding rates gave payroll workers from SMEs the opportunity to explain why their work processes required instant (not overnight) service on withholding rate queries for individuals, and this change was easily incorporated as the service was still under design.

SME participants state that their impression of the revenue body changes for the better: the Tax Administration is perceived as more "open" and "listening". At the same time, observers from the revenue body describe the tests as an invaluable source of insight about the taxpayers.

Low-threshold access to the test facility and empowerment of observers are two factors that contribute to a growing usability-testing culture at the Norwegian Tax Administration.

Source: Norwegian Tax Administration, *www.skatteetaten.no/en/International-pages/*

These efforts reflect an ambition to move towards more strategic and systematic approaches, which clearly resonated among workshop participants. They also respond to many of the issues identified in the survey and at the workshop, which are discussed in more detail in the next chapter offering guidance for successful implementation. On this background there would seem to be a compelling case for frameworks and practical guidance to support implementation as well as for setting up specific capabilities.

Formal mechanisms

It seems fairly common for revenue bodies to engage and involve taxpayers and stakeholders through formal mechanisms. One set of questions concerned the application of such mechanisms in the SME space. These questions addressed how revenue bodies engage and involve SME taxpayers and stakeholders in the design and implementation of major changes to the tax system and its administration, as well as how revenue bodies use forums or similar platforms to engage and involve SME taxpayers, the accountancy profession, and other stakeholders.

Consultation on major changes to the tax system and its administration

Survey responses reveal that most participating revenue bodies have formal consultation mechanisms or similar practices in relation to major changes to the tax system and its administration. In some cases consulting with stakeholders is a legal requirement, particularly as far as new legislation is concerned.

Generally the responsibility for conducting consultation on draft legislation resides with treasuries. Revenue bodies may, however, play a role in communicating the rationale and implications of intended policy changes to taxpayers and stakeholders as well as in channeling the views and ideas of taxpayers and stakeholders into the law-making process. It is also quite common for revenue bodies to consult with key stakeholders about the administrative aspects of new legislation. Often this will take place through forums or similar platforms for dialogue and co-operation.

Box 3.2 Generic Tax Policy Process in New Zealand

Inland Revenue engages with the public under what is known as the Generic Tax Policy Process. This approach was generated as part of an organisational review completed in 1994.

This process introduced a more robust five-stage process for public consultation when developing and introducing tax policy. This was based on the view that it is critical to have a tax policy framework that the private sector understands and buys into. Specific objectives were to encourage early consideration of key policy elements and trade-offs; to provide an opportunity for substantial external input; and to clarify accountabilities of participants in the process.

The five phases of the Generic Tax Policy Process are:

- **Strategic phase:** Economic, fiscal and revenue strategies;
- **Tactical phase:** 18 month work programme, consulted on, approved by Ministers, and published;
- **Operational phase:** Detailed design, communication, consultation, and Ministerial sign-off;
- **Legislative phase:** Legislative drafting, introduction of Bill, Select Committee process, passage of legislation, submissions and detailed officials' response; and
- **Implementation and review:** Post-implementation review and identification of remedials.

Consultation is incorporated throughout and it is important to emphasise that the approach to this consultation should be considered depending on the policy itself.

Source: Inland Revenue, *www.ird.govt.nz/*

One revenue body (New Zealand) provided an example of a generic consultation process comprising the whole policy cycle – see Box 3.2. This is consistent with the literature on co-production, which emphasises how clients and stakeholders may in principle be engaged and involved at all stages of the policy process (OECD, 2011).

A number of survey responses referred to the practical challenges involved in reaching beyond the largest and most articulate stakeholders. One revenue body (United Kingdom) provided an example detailing the steps taken to engage and involve the SME population in relation to a recent policy change affecting small businesses – see Box 3.3. This example illustrates how a tailored approach, taking account of some of the potential barriers to participation, may contribute to more meaningful and ultimately more effective engagement and involvement.

Box 3.3 Formal consultation in the United Kingdom

The vast majority of changes to UK tax law, including those affecting SMEs are the subject of formal consultation. Government does not consult on straightforward changes, revenue protection measures or areas where there is risk of forestalling. When it announces any new legislation, the Government publishes detailed notes with specific reference to the impact of the measure on small firms.

For the consultation document on simpler Income Tax for the simplest small businesses that was issued just after the 2012 Budget, the following steps were taken to consult the small business community:

- A short, business friendly stand-alone document was published on the HMRC website, outlining what the proposals mean for a small business and asking questions of particular interest to small businesses;
- HMRC worked with Business Link to include a note on its "what new" pages alerting small businesses to the consultation document and the stand alone business friendly version;
- HMRC used Twitter to publicise the proposals and provide a link to the Business Link page; and
- HMRC met with members of the Federation of Small Business and the Forum of Private Business (each representing over 100 000 small businesses) to discuss the proposals.

These activities contributed to raising awareness about the policy change and its implications for small businesses. HMRC has also taken significant steps in 2013 to complete a user-testing process with taxpayers who might benefit from this policy.

This work continues to inform the policy implementation. It has also been valuable in managing and satisfying concerns of internal and external stakeholders. Whilst no financial value can be directly attributed to such work, there clearly is added value to the pace of progress and overall outcome from the policy.

Separately, where significant changes are being made to the tax system, or when the department looks to develop its SME strategy, HMRC also consult with a wider array of SME representative organisations through their SME Overview Forum.

Source : Her Majesty's Revenue & Customs, *www.hmrc.gov.uk/*

Platforms for dialogue and co-operation

Most participating revenue bodies have established forums or similar formal platforms for dialogue and co-operation with key stakeholders, including SME representative bodies and the accountancy and advisory professions. These platforms allow for consultation on proposed changes to the tax system and its administration, as well as more general sharing of information, perspectives and intelligence. In some cases they have evolved into close working relationships where a high degree of collaboration takes place, as illustrated by some of the examples in Table 3.2.

Table 3.2 Platforms for dialogue and co-operation

Denmark – External Contact Committees and Simplification Advisory Forum	The External Contact Committees represent the main mechanism for engaging and involving Danish businesses and accountants. There is one central committee as well as six regional committees and six special committees focusing on specific areas like customs or VAT. In the committees, the ministry and administration consult with the main Danish associations representing businesses and accountants two to four times annually. The purpose is to inform about legislative and administrative initiatives as well as to discuss problems and possible improvements. A special forum consisting of representatives from the private sector and from public bodies was established in 2012 to advise government on initiatives to simplify regulation and reduce the administrative burden. Businesses and individuals can submit proposals on a website. These are then considered and elaborated by the forum before being submitted to the minister for the responsible area. The government is obliged to provide explanation if a suggestion cannot be accommodated.
France – Professional Panels and SME focus groups	The French Tax Administration is organising regular "professional committees" both on the central and local levels to discuss new developments and ideas in tax administration with SME representatives. A more recent initiative has been to "test" draft legislation with SME focus groups to be able to better take into account their views and ideas. A trial was conducted with a panel of 12 SME representatives for draft legislation on a new tax credit in favour of innovation and competitiveness. The focus group produced valuable feedback and the initiative was well received by the businesses involved.
Singapore – Taxpayer Feedback Panel	The Taxpayer Feedback Panel provides the IRAS with a channel to solicit input and feedback from taxpayers and stakeholders on new policies as well as administrative processes, services and initiatives. The panel consists of 20 members representing a broad range of professions and industry sectors. Each member serves a two-year term with the possibility of extending for a second term before the panel is renewed. A Mandarin panel was introduced in 2008 to reach out to the Chinese-speaking business community. Recent initiatives for which the panels have provided valuable input include a review of GST self-help material and a scheme to promote use of certified accounting software. The panels have also provided the IRAS with leverage in reaching out to the communities represented on the panels.
United Kingdom – Compliance Reform Forum	The Compliance Reform Forum (CRF) is made up of representatives from each of the recognised tax agent professional bodies. All new compliance initiatives are shared with this body, ideally before decisions are made, so that it can influence the design of the eventual product. The CRF meets three times a year, but its work is underpinned by a number of sub- groups allowing for in-depth discussion of the more significant initiatives. HMRC provide the Chair and Secretariat for CRF. Consultation with CRF and in particular the detailed work done in the sub-groups has led to better compliance products and better engagement with the accountancy profession.

Sources: SKAT: *www.skat.dk/SKAT.aspx?oID=44252*; French Tax Administration: *www.economie.gouv.fr/dgfip* ; Inland Revenue authority of Singapore: *www.iras.gov.sg/irashome/default.aspx*; Her Majesty's Revenue & Customs: *www.hmrc.gov.uk/consultations/crf.htm.*

Formal platforms of this kind provide a framework for building a strong relationship with SME representative bodies as well as bodies representing the accountancy and advisory professions. Revenue bodies may, however, still need more direct avenues for getting insights into the views and experience of individual SMEs, which may not always be accurately reflected by SME industry bodies or other stakeholders. An example from Australia (see

Box 3.4) shows how modern information and communication technologies can be used to create a platform for interaction with the large and heterogeneous SME population.

Box 3.4 Online SME community in Australia

The ATO operates a registration-based online community for SMEs with a turnover of between AUD 2 million and AUD 250 million.

The forum provides a unique opportunity for the ATO to engage directly with business operators and decision makers representing a diverse range of industries. Through discussions via this online community it is possible to gain a better understanding of the issues faced in the tax management of business. Identification of opportunities to reduce the cost of compliance, improve the administration of the tax system, and work with SMEs to improve products and strategies are key objectives of the forum. There are approximately 400 members who have signed up to the terms and conditions emphasising that any information covered on the site is not considered binding advice. Being online and available 24/7 makes participating easy and convenient for businesses and gives the ATO the opportunity for "real-time" information and feedback. Suggestions and feedback from members are presented to the relevant ATO areas.

The forum came about as a result of SME market research conducted in 2008, which led to an ambitious initiative to explore the relevance of social media for the SME market. The forum was designed with assistance from a market leader in private online communities, which continues to provide the platform. The forum is now managed and moderated exclusively by the ATO.

Activities include discussions, surveys, live chats with senior ATO leaders and educational webinars that include online presentations from ATO experts on topics of interest to SMEs. A recent webinar on Clean Energy attracted an audience of over 300 and a webinar on Fringe Benefits Tax and Entertainment over 800.

More information on the forum is available at its website: *www.ato-talkingtax.com.au*

In addition to the forums and similar mechanisms described above, revenue bodies have a range of other permanent or ad hoc mechanisms for consultation and co-operation with various stakeholders. These include (but are not limited to) other government agencies, labour representative bodies, research institutions and the academic community, organisations representing ethnic minorities, providers of third party data, and software developers.

Engaging and involving taxpayers and stakeholders in compliance activities

The preceding sections have dealt with what commitment revenue bodies have made to E&I approaches and what structures they have put in place to facilitate dialogue and co-operation with the most important stakeholder groups. Another way of approaching this would be to have a closer look at how E&I approaches are actually applied. This was the focus of another set of questions, which addressed how revenue bodies engage and involve SME taxpayers and stakeholders in the context of specific compliance activities.

This section will explore how revenue bodies engage and involve taxpayers and stakeholders in the context of specific compliance activities. The section follows the structure of the survey form, which distinguishes between three broad categories of compliance activities: information and guidance, compliance risk management, and systemic solutions. This typology is further explained under the individual headings below.

Information and guidance

Activities undertaken by revenue bodies to ensure that taxpayers are aware of tax obligations and are well equipped to comply with them are captured by the heading of *information and guidance*. These activities generally take place high up in the value chain in order to reduce the need for costlier and less effective interventions at a later stage. They are also important from a service perspective, as they are about facilitating compliance.

Survey responses reveal that most participating revenue bodies seek to engage and involve taxpayers and stakeholders in some way in their information and guidance activities – see Table 3.3 for some illustrative examples. Among the most frequently cited applications are quantitative and qualitative social research (for instance surveys, focus groups and interviews) to seek input from users or get their feedback on new or existing products.

Table 3.3 Engaging & Involving in information and guidance

Australia – Digital tools for small businesses	The ATO offers a suite of digital tools to support SMEs in managing their tax affairs. These tools have been developed with input and feedback from business owners and the accountancy profession. A recent example is a tool to help calculating capital gains tax liability. The tool was developed through a series of facilitated sessions with business owners and tax practitioners. Feedback whilst prototyping the solutions showed that most business owners would involve a tax practitioner. This led to the tool being tailored more to the needs of tax practitioners based on findings from these sessions.
Chile – Co-design of web portal	The Chilean Tax Service collaborated with two major industry bodies to develop a web portal to strengthen accounting and tax compliance among small businesses. The portal offers targeted information and guidance, systems for electronic invoicing, simplified and complete accounting systems, functionality to consolidate data and calculate tax liabilities, and an interface for electronic filing. The collaboration with industry bodies helped tailor the product to better meet the needs and expectations of the target group. It also provided the revenue body with leverage in promoting the portal, as the trade confederations provide instructors and organise training seminars.
Singapore – Enhancing GST Assisted Self-Help Kit	The IRAS is enhancing its GST Assisted Self-Help Kit based on input and feedback from taxpayers and stakeholders. The original toolkit was introduced in 2010 to support businesses in reviewing the accuracy of their GST submissions, but take-up was slow and feedback indicated that it was not user-friendly. The IRAS therefore solicited feedback from a sample of businesses using the kit, from tax agents through existing consultation mechanisms, and from the Taxpayer Feedback Panel. The insights and ideas derived from this exercise will enable the IRAS to develop an enhanced kit better tailored to the needs of the target group.
United Kingdom – Toolkits to reduce error	The HMRC engaged the tax agent community to clarify opportunities to support them in their efforts to submit accurate and timely returns. One of the priorities agreed was that the HMRC should provide a range of toolkits addressing the most common errors. Tax agents were invited to contribute to this work as part of the project team, feedback to toolkits was sought through existing consultation mechanisms, and the toolkits were tested with end-users at in-house workshops and by an external agency. The 20 resulting toolkits have been downloaded more than 250,000 times, and the HMRC estimate that they have prevented the loss of over GBP 100 million over a three-year period.

Engaging and involving taxpayers and stakeholders can in principle contribute to enhancing any information and guidance product. Survey responses, examples and discussions at the workshop illustrate that revenue bodies have sought input and feedback from taxpayers and stakeholders for products ranging from letters, leaflets and online guidance material over presentations, seminars, webinars and videos to sometimes fairly sophisticated digital tools.

As illustrated by the examples featured in the table above, however, the examples documented in more detail tend to cluster around digital tools and toolkits allowing the revenue body to reach out on a one-to-many basis. The strategy of working with stakeholders to better leverage on technology is also very pronounced for systemic solutions, which is explored later in this chapter.

Some revenue bodies are also seeking more far-reaching forms of collaboration involving a greater role for taxpayers and stakeholders in the design and delivery of information and guidance. An example of this was provided by the HMRC in the United Kingdom – see Box 3.5.

Box 3.5 Education Partnering in the United Kingdom

The HMRC has adopted a partnership-based approach – known as the SME Education Partnering Strategy – to providing information and guidance to SMEs that are either unaware of their tax obligations or needs help to comply with them.

Reaching the estimated 700,000 SMEs in this sub-segment (many of which are uncomfortable about dealing with authorities) requires a leveraged one-to-many approach. Working with and through SME industry bodies and intermediaries allows the HMRC to benefit from their knowledge, reach and credibility, including by drawing on their networks and communication channels.

The strategy has particular focus on key business life events like starting a business, registering for VAT, taking on an employee, and ceasing to trade. Among the products and services offered are modular e-learning packages, pre-recorded or live webinars, YouTube videos, presentations and workshops. The programme is coordinated by a national team supported by regional and local staff. Each partner has a dedicated single point of contact responsible for developing the relationship and providing the partner with a channel for feedback.

The HMRC estimate (based on modelled assumptions) that these activities prevent over GBP one million a month being lost through error. Research is being conducted to further document effectiveness and identify opportunities for improvement. Early indications are that the programme contributes to a significant uplift in awareness about tax obligations and the ability to comply with them.

It is expected that the programme will be expanded over the next four-year period.

Revenue bodies may also derive considerable savings from avoiding investment in services that do not meet the needs or expectations of the intended end-users. Sweden reported how workshops to further develop a "service declaration" (involving commitment to clearly defined service standards) led to the idea being scrapped, as it did not have enough traction with taxpayers. Similarly in Denmark, the idea of teaching young people about taxes were scrapped after interviews with the target group indicated that interest was limited.

While these examples of sunk costs avoided by engaging and involving taxpayers and stakeholders at an early stage are from information and guidance, the same principles would apply in principle in any area, and the potential savings would seem to be proportional with the budgets involved.

Compliance risk management activities

Even the best designed and executed information and guidance activities will not be enough to mitigate all compliance risks. Activities intended to address intentional and unintentional error further down the value chain are captured under the heading of *compliance risk management activities.*

Survey responses reveal that many of the participating revenue bodies are exploring the potential of E&I approaches in the context of compliance risk management activities. Applications include engagement with taxpayers and stakeholders to identify risks, better understand behaviours, or design cost-effective interventions. Revenue bodies may also seek leverage from stakeholders (who are often better positioned to influence taxpayers) in the actual implementation of interventions. Some of the more far-reaching approaches involve a delegation of regulatory responsibilities in return for transparency and reassurance on risk management frameworks and capabilities.

Frequently the engagement and involvement of taxpayers and stakeholders in compliance activities is (at least in part) coordinated through existing platforms for consultation and collaboration. The IRAS for instance work with industry bodies and the Taxpayer Feedback Panels to ensure that the proposed treatments are proportionate to the risks, targeted at the right sub-segments, and practical in view of the industry context. Similarly, in the United Kingdom, the HMRC has used the Compliance Reform Forum to engage tax agents, SME industry bodies and the voluntary sector in the design, implementation and evaluation of treatments.

Table 3.4 Integrating with compliance risk management methodologies

Australia – Compliance Effectiveness Methodology	The ATO has developed the Compliance Effectiveness Methodology to assist risk managers in planning, implementing and evaluating treatments. The use of the methodology provides taxpayers and stakeholders with a number of opportunities to be involved in the tax compliance management process. The methodology requires risk managers to identify behaviours and their drivers. This kind of research may involve surveys or other forms of user research. Once behavioural drivers have been identified, respective treatments are developed. Often specific tactical solutions (such as letters to the community) are collaboratively designed and usability tested with a sample group of the people who may be affected. Indicators of success come from internal quantitative data (such as revenue collection figures) but may also be identified through qualitative feedback mechanisms such as perception surveys, consultative forum feedback, interviews or visits by tax officers.
Denmark – Guidelines for treatment projects	The guidelines for designing and implementing treatment projects in the Danish Tax and Customs Administration recommend that risk managers systematically consider opportunities for engaging and involving taxpayers and stakeholders. The guidelines recommend starting from a detailed analysis of the target group and stakeholders, which are not limited to SME representative bodies and the accountancy profession, but may in principle include anyone positioned to influence the compliance risk in question. It is further suggested that early contact with taxpayers and stakeholders can enhance the understanding of the risk and the opportunities for cost-effectively addressing it, including by revealing shared interests and possibilities for co-operation.

In principle E&I approaches may, as discussed in the last chapter, be applied at all phases of the compliance risk management cycle: risk identification, analysis and prioritisation, and treatment design, implementation and evaluation. A number of revenue bodies have on this background taken steps to integrate E&I approaches in the methodologies supporting their compliance risk management activities – see Table 3.4 for some illustrative examples.

Experience from other areas of the public sector has suggested that engaging and involving taxpayers and stakeholders may enhance accountability and democratic governance (OECD, 2011). In this context it is interesting to note that the National Tax Service of Korea has set up an external panel overseeing audit selection. A 2007 survey showed that 73.2% of the general public felt that this mechanism contribute to enhancing objectivity and transparency in tax audits.

Even when a business has been selected for audit there may still be opportunities for engaging and involving it to secure a better outcome and/or reduce costs. An example from Ireland (see Box 3.6) shows how case management procedures can be adapted to involve SMEs in the case resolution and to focus dialogue on future compliance – in effect enhancing a well-known instrument by adding an E&I component to it.

Box 3.6 Revised case management procedures in Ireland

Revenue in Ireland has revised case management procedures in order to complement traditional audits with other interventions relying more on dialogue.

As part of the new procedures, SMEs can be contacted in advance of an audit and invited to examine their records and returns in relation to a specific risk with a view to making a voluntary disclosure. Larger companies can be invited to make a full self-examination, which together with Revenue's risk assessment will form the basis for dialogue on measures to improve compliance.

These new and evolving types of interventions make SMEs more aware of their responsibilities and afford both sides a platform to manage compliance risks in cost-effective ways.

Survey responses, examples and discussions at the workshops suggest that engaging and involving taxpayers and stakeholders offers a broad range of options other than audits – see Table 3.5 for some illustrative examples. Revenue bodies seem to have been particularly active in working with stakeholders to improve their understanding of the risks and tailor the treatments accordingly, or to leverage on the knowledge, reach, credibility and efforts of stakeholders during the actual implementation.

Table 3.5 Engaging & Involving in compliance risk management activities

Canada – Consumer awareness campaign	The CRA has worked with the Canadian Home Builders Association (CHBA) to develop and deliver a campaign to raise consumer awareness about risks related to buying services in the underground economy. The campaign brand and slogan "Get it in writing" emphasised the significant risks incurred by consumers who chose to buy house renovation services in the underground economy where they enjoy no warranties or legal protection. While the CRA funded the three-year campaign and worked with the CHBA on some of the high-level messages, the CHBA had the lead role in design and delivery, as public opinion research indicated that this would increase the impact. The CRA in other words relied on the knowledge, reach, credibility and efforts of an industry representative body to drive in a wedge between consumers and providers of services in the underground economy. The original campaign is now finished, but the CRA continue to use the campaign material with the permission of the CHBA.
New Zealand – Partnerships with SME representative bodies in high-risk industries	Inland Revenue in New Zealand is forming partnerships with SME representative bodies in high-risk industries as part of a ten-year programme to tackle the underground economy. Inland Revenue for instance approached SME representative bodies in the hospitality industry following the identification of this as a high-risk area. This has contributed to a better understanding of the risks, the underlying drivers, and the possibilities for intervention. It has also helped identify shared interests and opportunities for further collaboration.
Sweden – Co-operation with large contractors	The Swedish Tax Agency is collaborating with principal contractors to enhance compliance among subcontractors. The contractors formally commit to enhancing compliance in their supply chain, and the revenue body provides support for the tendering process, including tax information on potential subcontractors and information on international taxation issues arising from the use of subcontractors based abroad. The revenue body also collaborates with SME representative bodies to address some of the specific compliance issues among the subcontractors. The programme, which involves about 30 FTEs, affects about 250 contractors and about 400 projects involving a large number of SME subcontractors.

These examples relate to partnership-based approaches addressing high-risk industries. These approaches, acknowledging that the risks and issues are too big and too complex to be effectively addressed by the revenue body alone, explore shared interests with stakeholders to achieve synergies and leverage. These partnering approaches are echoed in an example from Norway (see Box 3.7) where collaboration with stakeholders has evolved into a formal platform for addressing the underground economy.

Box 3.7 Alliance against the underground economy in Norway

The Norwegian Tax Administration, recognising that it has limited reach on its own, has formed an alliance with key stakeholders to better address the underground economy.

The alliance – consisting of the Norwegian Association of Local and Regional Authorities, the main confederations of trade unions, the Confederation of Norwegian Enterprise and the Norwegian Tax Administration – is focused on joint preventive efforts to combat the underground economy. It was originally formed in 1997 and has since evolved into an enduring partnership.

The basis for the partnership is a shared concern for tax revenues, the prevention of undesirable distortion of competition, and the securing of sound working conditions. All parties recognise that by working together they achieve significant leverage for their respective agendas.

All partners in the alliance contribute to developing the two-year action plan. Stable activities are school visits, information material, information visits, public meetings, and campaigns. These activities are complemented with visible enforcement activities leveraged by press coverage.

Highlights from the action plan for 2012-14 include two awareness raising campaigns. The first is a continuation of a well-established campaign targeting young people aged 17-18 years in order to affect their norms before they go on to become consumers, trades-people or business owners. Over the last seven years, this campaign has engaged more than 200.000 students (or the equivalent of 60% of the age-group) in classroom discussions on taxes and public goods. Evaluations show that the campaign has a positive impact on norms.

The other campaign is directed at consumers and aims to raise awareness around the benefits of trading "over the counter", the importance of obtaining receipts and invoices, and the requirements for electronic payments for some transactions. The campaign is supported by a web application allowing consumers to check whether a business is registered and assess (based on a range of simple criteria) whether it is reliable.

The alliance offers the revenue body a stronger platform for launching activities directed at the underground economy. The alliance has its own website (in addition to campaign websites) and its own visual identity containing the logos of stakeholders next to the message that "the underground economy is a thief".

The Norwegian Tax Administration has found that its messages are more readily accepted by businesses, trades-people and consumers when embraced by stakeholders like industry representative bodies.

The Swedish example illustrates how principal contractors may be relied upon to enhance compliance among their subcontractors. By collaborating with the principal contractors and by designing enforcement activities to raise attention around the risks and issues involved, the revenue body has altered the compliance dynamics in a high-risk industry. The same principles are explored in an example from Denmark (see Box 3.8), where the revenue body has produced a toolkit to assist principal contractors in the cleaning industry.

These examples are notable for identifying and exploiting opportunities for collaboration that create value to both the revenue body and the stakeholder. Interested organisations need to build a profile for themselves and deliver value to their constituency. Principal contractors generally have an interest in using honest and reliable subcontractors. Industry bodies have an interest in securing a level playing field for their constituency, safeguarding the reputation of the industry, and keeping the administrative burden low. And consumers want to enjoy warranties and legal protection – especially in relation to major investments in their home. These shared or compatible interests open up possibilities for collaboration to the benefit of all parties involved.

Box 3.8 Collaboration with principal contractors in Denmark

The Danish Tax and Customs Administration are collaborating with principal contractors to address the extensive use of unregistered labour among subcontractors in the cleaning industry. In the experience of the revenue body, significant problems with unregistered labour are encountered at about one third of work sites inspected.

In addition to lost revenue, the extensive use of unregistered labour leads to unfair competition among sub-contractors and reputation risks for the principal contractors, which are often public bodies or well-reputed private companies.

The revenue body approached principal contractors to raise awareness about the risk of being associated with unregistered labour, and to suggest a possible solution to the problem. The solution proposed was a toolkit developed in collaboration with stakeholder representatives, offering a set of principles for principal contractors to consider when concluding contracts with subcontractors. These include limiting the number of subcontractors, imposing requirements for ID cards and uniforms, and provisions to request proof of identity or documentation for paid withholding taxes.

The revenue body has complemented this initiative with conventional audits leveraged by media coverage, which has further increased awareness of the problem.

Principal contractors have responded positively to the initiative. In the first year of operation, the principles The principles have been implemented for contracts worth EUR 300 million.

A common perception that also came up in the course of this project is that E&I approaches are most suited for compliant taxpayers and may be misplaced for other segments. The examples above, however, illustrate how engaging and involving stakeholders can provide leverage for interventions directed at high-risk industries. These examples strongly suggest that E&I approaches are in fact *particularly well suited* for dealing with the complex dynamics surrounding intentional non-compliance where traditional approaches have often failed to deliver the desired outcomes.

An example from Australia (see Box 3.9) adds further credibility to this argument. The example illustrates how publishing benchmarks reflecting industry norms can put pressure on businesses that do not have legitimate reasons for falling outside the norms. The benchmarks also provide another stakeholder, the accountancy profession, with important leverage in performing their role.

Box 3.9 Australian Small Business Benchmarks

The ATO is using comparative income and expense ratio benchmarks to increase visibility around norms in a range of industries.

The benchmarks, which were developed with input from SME representative bodies, reflect actual information reported by SME taxpayers and are grouped by industry classifications and turnover ranges. A statistical band of values above and below the average for each industry and turnover range is published, reflecting that there are legitimate commercial variances amongst comparable businesses. The published values allow individual businesses to compare their incomes to expenses ratio against their industry peers.

This visibility around norms may prompt businesses reporting disproportionately low income to take self-corrective action. At the same time, businesses operating within the band of values for their industry can have increased confidence that they are operating on a level playing field and that the ATO is acting on those outside the benchmark ranges.

The benchmarks also provide an effective platform for dialogue with individual taxpayers, industry bodies, and the accountancy profession, as well as for mass communication to raise awareness about compliance risks. They also provide tax agents with leverage in opening up potentially sensitive conversations with clients on variations from industry norms.

Tracking of effectiveness shows significant increases in the number of businesses reporting income in the same range as their industry peers. In 2009-10 the ATO wrote to 30,000 businesses that were reporting outside of their industry norm. In the following year, 17% of these businesses reported income within their industry norm without further intervention by the ATO.

Some accountants in Australia are now reporting that they use the benchmarks to assist clients in sales or acquisitions of businesses. This seems to indicate more general acceptance of the benchmarks and an additional valuable outcome for the community.

Some of the more far-reaching approaches involve a delegation of regulatory responsibilities in return for transparency and reassurance on risk management frameworks and capabilities. This is illustrated by an example from the Netherlands (see Box 3.10) where the revenue body has collaborated with the accountancy profession and industry bodies to design a system of meta-monitoring based on their experience with "horizontal monitoring" of large businesses.

The example is noteworthy for lifting the perspective from the individual return. Instead the object of control becomes the system producing the returns, and the purpose of the control to provide reassurance that the system can be relied upon to produce correct returns. This allows the revenue body to shift resources to taxpayers whose systems are deemed less reliable and SMEs to focus on their business. At the same time the important role of intermediaries in bringing about correct returns is acknowledged and reinforced.

Similar arrangements are being considered by a number of other revenue bodies. The Swedish Tax Administration has worked with the accountancy profession to develop a concept linking the risk-rating of businesses to quality assurance processes overseen by the professional body of accountants. This provides an additional incentive for accountants to review and improve quality assurance processes and for businesses to sign up with accountants complying with the standards promoted by their professional body. The French Tax Administration is preparing to pilot a new relationship with businesses with a similar strategic intent: to develop a relationship with businesses based on trust, and to offer legal certainty in return for transparency and reassurance about the quality of the processes behind the tax returns.

Box 3.10 Meta-monitoring of SMEs in the Netherlands

The Netherlands Tax and Customs Administration has introduced horizontal monitoring for SMEs in 2008. After a pilot period the concept has been implemented on a larger scale since 2011. The essence of the concept is that compliance agreements are signed with tax intermediary organisations. Under the working of the covenant, intermediaries file tax returns on behalf of their clients which are subject to controls that ensure the quality of the tax return. If specific fiscal issues would arise the tax intermediary is bound, under to covenant, to discuss this with the revenue body before filing the tax return. The benefits for the SME and for the tax intermediary are a better relationship with the revenue body, more speedy procedures and more certainty on their tax position, and less audits. Part of the system is that the revenue body performs a limited number of audits and reviews as a reality check, i.e. checking whether the system is working as intended and the tax returns filed under the covenant are correct. This system is referred to as meta-monitoring.

In the Platform on Horizontal Monitoring the revenue body discusses the developments on horizontal monitoring with the organisations of tax intermediaries who participate in the horizontal monitoring programme and the professional bodies. This platform is the place where parties involved in horizontal monitoring can exchange ideas en experiences and stimulate the further development of the programme, based on co-creation.

In 2012 the intermediary organisations expressed their concern on how the revenue body was implementing the meta-monitoring in practice. Their membership argued that they had the impression that they faced more audits, instead of less audits. The revenue body indicated that the number of audits under the horizontal monitoring programme was far less than in the traditional way of working. But in individual cases some tax intermediaries had other experience and of course this affected the business case for horizontal monitoring. Parties in the Platform agreed that it was necessary to solve this issue together. A joint working group of revenue body officials and representatives of the tax intermediaries worked out a new approach for meta-monitoring. The revenue body felt some discomfort embarking on this co-design road, as in the end, it will be held accountable for a sufficient level of monitoring activities. But at the same time tax intermediaries of course challenged the revenue body on its commitment to really work on a co-operative basis.

The outcome was that the working group came up with a solution which encompassed a more comprehensive approach entailing not just traditional audits, but also making better use of the control mechanisms already implemented by tax intermediaries. This actually strengthened the meta-monitoring while at the same time articulating the benefits of the horizontal monitoring programme for tax intermediaries and their clients.

Systemic solutions

The ideal way of managing compliance risks is to introduce lasting changes to the compliance environment eliminating or dramatically reducing the need for activities further down the value chain. This is what is implied by the term *systemic solutions*. By shifting activities up the value chain, revenue bodies can permanently free resources for addressing risks that still require direct interventions. In this way a focus on systemic solutions may not only lead to improved compliance outcomes and improved service experiences, but also to a more optimal allocation of resources.

Survey responses reveal a growing focus on systemic solutions. Many of the participating revenue bodies emphasise the importance of systemic solutions, and it is widely acknowledged that engaging and involving taxpayers and stakeholders can contribute in a range of ways, and that some systemic solutions will only be possible with the contribution of taxpayers and stakeholders.

Participating revenue bodies all acknowledge that feedback from taxpayers and stakeholders can help identify "friction points" and opportunities for improvements also at the systemic level. This feedback may originate in forums and other formal mechanisms for consultation and collaboration, come about as a result of other E&I activities, or originate from other sources. An example provided by Korea (see Box 3.11) illustrates how complaints and other feedback can be used to drive improvement while also enhancing customer satisfaction.

Box 3.11 Listening to taxpayers and stakeholders in Korea

The National Tax Service of Korea has set up a system to channel complaints, compliments and suggestions from taxpayers into improvement processes.

The system, which is known as the Voice of Customer Total Management System, is intended to identify opportunities for improving the service experience as well as the performance of the tax system as a whole by systematically analysing feedback. The feedback, regardless of the originating channel, is processed at a Customer Satisfaction Centre. The average processing time has been 26 hours. Taxpayers and stakeholders are notified by SMS on the results. Taxpayer satisfaction with the system was 92 out of a possible 100 in 2011.

More than 160,000 feedback instances were processed between July 2008 and December 2011, leading to almost 500 improvement opportunities being pursued. This has resulted in systemic solutions like raised threshold for advance VAT payments, improvements to the online VAT filing interface, and upgrades to the system for settlement of payroll tax at the end of the year.

At the same time the system contributes to increased satisfaction and to building trust in the revenue body.

Complaints are (like disputes) a form of "failure signals" indicating that something has gone wrong from the perspective of the taxpayer. The example shows how these failure signals can be turned into a resource for the revenue body. Acting on such failure signals is critical for satisfaction, trust and procedural justice, which all is known to impact on voluntary compliance. Research indicates that respectful treatment is more important to clients than the actual outcome of a dispute, which would also indicate that authorities can gain trust simply by showing they are genuinely concerned about the experience of clients (Braithwaite, 2008; Tyler, 2001).

While explicitly linking systemic solutions to the management of compliance risks and issues is a relatively new development, many revenue bodies provided examples, perhaps reflecting that this is perceived to be an innovative and promising area. The examples range from consultation on changes to forms and processes over collaboration on digital interfaces or systems integration to formal partnerships on standards for accounting solutions and POS systems. Most of the examples leverage in some way on technology – see Table 3.6 for illustrative examples.

A striking feature of these examples is that they all seek in some way to leverage on technology to embed compliance as a more likely "default" outcome of the process starting with the individual transaction and ending with filing and payment. Because this process is in large part external to the revenue body, the understanding of it or the ability to influence it is significantly enhanced (and indeed sometimes only made possible) by the participation of taxpayers and stakeholders. Collaboration as a consequence tends to deepen when the object for improvement is (in whole or in part) external to the revenue body.

Table 3.6. Systemic solutions leveraging on technology

Canada – Enhanced functionality of digital interface	The CRA is enhancing its MyBusinessAccount digital interface for businesses after consultation with tax practitioners showed that they would appreciate the ability to view certain calculations on the CIT return online. The changes will contribute to reducing the administrative burden and enhancing voluntary compliance.
Chile – Promoting electronic invoicing	The Chilean Tax Service is collaborating with large businesses to promote the use of electronic invoicing among SMEs. Large taxpayers signing up to the programme commit to promoting electronic invoicing among their suppliers, and to work with the revenue body to provide these with information and training. So far 28 large businesses have signed up for the programme, which affects a large and growing number of SMEs.
Ireland – Introduction of electronic system for withholding tax	Revenue in Ireland has involved software developers, industry bodies and principal contractors to prepare for the introduction of an electronic system for withholding tax. The system, which affects primarily the construction sector, is intended to improve compliance and reduce the administrative burden falling on both businesses and the revenue body. During the development phase, Revenue made presentations to intended end-users, and their feedback led to a range of changes and transitional measures.
Netherlands – Certification of POS systems and cloud-based bookkeeping	The Netherlands Tax and Customs Administration is working with stakeholders to improve the quality and reliability of cloud-based accounting solutions and POS systems respectively. In both cases this started out as dialogue with software developers, the accountancy profession and SME representative bodies. This led to the creation of partnerships where key stakeholders work together to establish and promote certified standards. These standards will in turn contribute to standardising the administrative chain and provide reassurance around POS transactions.
New Zealand – Tax Agents B2B Web Service	New Zealand Inland Revenue collaborated with software developers and tax agents to develop a web solution facilitating the sharing of data between SMEs and their tax agents. The resulting Tax Agents B2B Web Service provides tax agents with a view of their client's transactions for all linked tax types (except PAYE and related taxes) on a daily basis and allows for the transfer of this data into their agency software.
Singapore – Simplified filing for small businesses	The IRAS has worked with SMEs and tax agents to simplify filing procedures for small businesses. Feedback revealed that the existing form was too complicated and contained many items that did not apply to small businesses, which found it difficult to complete without the assistance of tax agents. To remedy this situation a significantly shortened online form was developed and filing procedures were simplified. This solution was based in part on suggestions from small business representatives and tax agents, which also contributed to pilot-testing before the initiative was rolled out full-scale.

Among the applied strategies are improved recording of transactions, promotion of electronic invoicing, improved accounting systems, simplified filing procedures, integration of revenue body systems with accounting systems used by taxpayers and their intermediaries, enhanced functionality of revenue body systems, and expanded withholding regimes for high-risk industries. Taxpayers and stakeholders provide critical insights in the design phase and sometimes leverage for the implementation itself. The Chilean example where principal contractors promote e-invoicing among their subcontractors (echoing examples in the last section) is one example of how mutual interests can be explored.

The Dutch examples with certification of POS systems and cloud-based accounting solutions respectively, illustrate how revenue bodies may collaborate with the developers and providers of the vital infrastructure underpinning SME compliance. In the digital age the nature of this infrastructure is changing. An example from Denmark (see Box 3.12) provides a vision for how these developments may be explored by revenue bodies to radically alter the way SMEs do business and interact with the revenue body.

Box 3.12 Concept for automated processes in Denmark

The tax gap for small businesses constitutes a significant part of the total SME tax gap in Denmark. Random audits indicate that close to three quarters of the SME tax gap relate to businesses with less than 10 employees.

This situation prompted the Danish Tax and Customs Administration to think about opportunities for radical innovation. The revenue body used lead user innovation methodology to develop a new concept to improve the quality of bookkeeping. A total of 14 lead users representing major trends in society were charged with rethinking how SMEs do business and interact with the revenue body.

The project resulted in a concept for fully automating the process from individual transactions to the final tax return. The central idea is an automatic flow of information about transactions between the business, its bank connection, the accounting system and the revenue body. As a result the owners of small businesses will no longer need to understand (or worry about) complex tax rules. Instead they will be able to focus on what they do best while the revenue body will have higher reassurance about the quality of their returns.

The concept is now being refined and prototyped with some of the lead users. Collaboration between banks, accounting systems suppliers and the revenue body's IT developers is also taking place to discuss implications for legislation, IT systems and administrative processes. The final concept is expected to be ready for presentation in the autumn of 2013.

These examples illustrate how technological developments raise the prospect of radically rethinking the processes behind SME compliance. Revenue bodies may work with SME taxpayers and other stakeholders to co-create systems providing SMEs and revenue body alike with a shared and real-time view of the businesses results, the taxes and repayments that are due and a mutual assurance that the figures can be relied upon. That development would realise in the SME segment the principles that underlie co-operative compliance strategies for the large business segment – in exchange for transparency business achieves certainty and lower compliance costs.

Overall picture emerging

This chapter has reviewed current and emerging practices. It is clear that revenue bodies engage and involve taxpayers and stakeholders in a range of ways. This is expressed in formal commitment, efforts to build frameworks and capabilities, and a range of fairly consolidated mechanisms for consultation and collaboration. Examples across the areas of information and guidance, compliance risk management and systemic solutions illustrate how revenue bodies have sought input from taxpayers and stakeholders, responded to feedback, and collaborated on a range of matters and initiatives where win-win situations existed or could be created.

This section will highlight some of the findings on the overall experience before lifting the perspective to discuss some of the broader lessons emerging out of the chapter.

Overall experience with compliance activities

Engaging and involving taxpayers and stakeholders seem most mainstreamed for information and guidance. Most revenue bodies are taking advantage of social research or user-testing methodologies to tailor the services offered to the needs and expectations of taxpayers and stakeholders. Many revenue bodies are also actively collaborating with stakeholders like intermediaries and SME industry bodies to design or deliver these services, and in some cases formal partnerships have been established.

Examples from compliance risk management show that revenue bodies engage and involve taxpayers and stakeholders to some extent during all phases of the risk management cycle. This is especially true as far as improving the understanding of the risks, tailoring treatments, or seeking leverage for the interventions is concerned. Involving taxpayers and stakeholders in risk identification and prioritisation, detailed treatment design, and evaluation is less common, although it may be meaningful in particular circumstances – for instance in the context of partnership-based efforts to address high-risk industries, as illustrated by some examples.

Revenue bodies also increasingly engage and involve taxpayers and stakeholders in the context of systemic solutions. It is widely acknowledged that making lasting changes to the compliance environment is preferable to downstream management of risks and issues, and that such systemic solutions are often enhanced or indeed made possible by the participation of taxpayers and stakeholders. Examples range from consultation on changes to forms and processes over collaboration on digital interfaces or systems integration, to formal partnerships on standards for accounting solutions and POS systems.

Engagement and leverage strategies

Looking across survey responses, examples provided and discussions at the workshop, it is possible to establish some fundamental differences in how taxpayers and stakeholders have been engaged and involved. It is also possible to identify what stakeholders have been involved and what leverage strategies have been applied.

Individual SME taxpayers are generally engaged and involved on an ad hoc basis with emphasis on information and consultation, for instance to improve the understanding of a risk or tailor a product or an intervention. Some examples also illustrate the potential for engaging and involving SME taxpayers in more innovative ways. This can for instance be as part of an intervention where they may be required to co-produce the outcome by performing a self-review, which will serve as a basis for discussions with the revenue body focusing on future compliance.

Stakeholders generally command more resources and are better positioned to invest in a long-term relationship. Therefore it makes good sense that stakeholders are often engaged and involved in more deliberate ways involving a higher degree of collaboration (including co-creation and co-production) and sometimes leading to lasting partnerships and alliances.

The stakeholders identified can be clustered in six categories: intermediaries, industry bodies, other government bodies, civil society, SME business partners, and stakeholders in the compliance chain (see Figure 3.1). These stakeholders often are better positioned than the revenue body to either directly influence the behaviour of SME taxpayers or influence critical factors in the compliance environment. They may also command critical knowledge or perspectives that can enhance revenue body strategies, activities and solutions.

Figure 3.1 Stakeholders in SME compliance

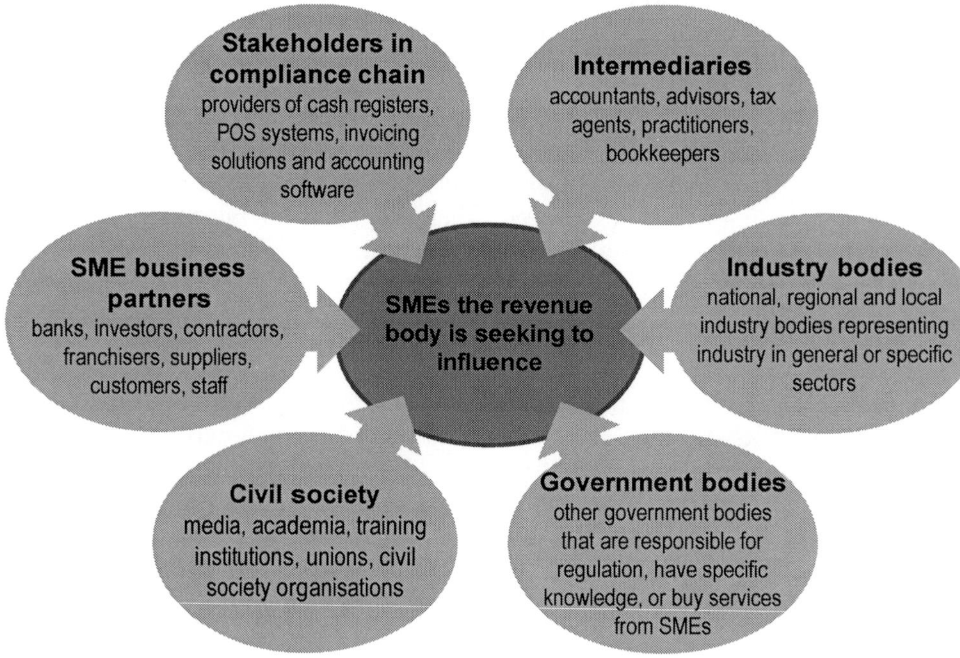

Revenue bodies have most experience with engaging and involving intermediaries and industry bodies. There also are some good examples of collaborating with stakeholders in the SME compliance chain (notably developers and vendors of accounting solutions and POS systems) on systemic solutions, which seems to be an emerging trend driven in part by an increased understanding of the role of technology. Finally there would seem to be significant potential for further collaboration with SME business partners, civil society, and (paradoxically) other government bodies.

The leverage strategies applied depend on the particular stakeholder, the risk or issue addressed, and the specific circumstances. They also often occur in combination with two or more strategies overlapping and reinforcing each other or as components of broader initiatives. It is, however, still possible to identify patterns suggesting some potential "generic" strategies that may be adjusted to different contexts and circumstances:

- **Stakeholder leverage:** leveraging on the knowledge, reach, credibility and efforts of stakeholders, for instance in the form of the stakeholder endorsing the messages of the revenue body or substituting or complementing revenue body efforts;

- **Intelligence leverage:** leveraging on knowledge and data held by stakeholders that may contribute to identifying patterns or cases, and may feed into products, interventions and solutions as well as inform other leverage strategies;
- **Norms leverage:** leveraging from raising visibility around norms to enhance self-regulation, for instance by creating visibility around norms or deliberately framing messages to reinforce positive norms and marginalise undesired behaviours;
- **Media leverage:** leveraging on media to enhance awareness about tax obligations, revenue body service offerings, and the risks associated with non-compliance, as well as to reinforce positive norms; and
- **Technology leverage:** leveraging on technology to facilitate flows of information and data, automate processes, improve service offerings, and embed compliance as the default option or increase the risks associated with non-compliance.

While these strategies (excepting the first) are perfectly feasible without stakeholder engagement, they are clearly enhanced by collaborating with stakeholders. Revenue bodies may for instance design systemic solutions leveraging on technology on their own, but the quality of the solutions and their impact is likely to be greatly enhanced by engaging and involving stakeholders.

These five strategies may along with the six stakeholder categories shown above, serve as a checklist for revenue bodies to assess whether they have considered relevant stakeholders and potential leverage strategies in the context of a particular strategy or initiative.

Revenue body experience indicates that E&I approaches work best and lead to the best results when taxpayers and stakeholders are involved at an early stage – ideally right from the beginning of a project when the search for solutions has not yet begun. Taxpayers and stakeholders have different perspectives that will affect how a problem is framed and what solutions will seem appropriate. Bringing in these perspectives at an early stage will challenge assumptions, ensure that solutions are tailored, and enhance ownership. Some examples illustrate how this has added significant value or led to low-value solutions being abandoned before big investments were made.

Final observations

Revenue body experience with E&I approaches is encouraging. Drawing on the input of taxpayers and stakeholders is fairly mainstreamed, particularly as far as information and guidance is concerned. In addition to formal consultation mechanisms for major initiatives, there also are a range of platforms for consultation and collaboration, and some revenue bodies are putting in place systematic approaches and developing specialist capabilities. Revenue bodies also increasingly collaborate with stakeholders to achieve leverage for their activities and sometimes this leads to the formation of lasting partnerships. Some of the more far-reaching approaches involve a delegation of regulatory responsibilities (in return for reassurance about the quality of the returns) or the co-creation of systemic solutions substituting revenue body efforts.

While the rationale for these strategies is clear, and the overall experience encouraging, few examples include robust evaluation setups allowing for benefits to be firmly established. Most examples are instead underpinned by plausible (if implicit) assumptions and their impact illustrated with reference to improved outputs (for instance a simplified procedure or an improved product) or positive feedback. There would therefore seem to be significant potential for further developing or articulating the underlying programme theory, linking it to reliable indicators allowing for the tracking of outcomes, and quantifying the benefits by sensitivity analysis and other means.

Bibliography

Braithwaite, V. (2008), "Tax Evasion" in M. Tonry (ed.): *Handbook on Crime and Public Policy*, Oxford University Press, Oxford.

OECD (2004), *Compliance Risk Management: Managing and Improving Tax Compliance*, Forum on Tax Administration, OECD, Paris. *www.oecd.org/tax/taxadministration/33818656.pdf*

OECD (2011a), *Together for Better Public Services: Partnering with Citizens and Civil Society*, OECD Public Governance Reviews, OECD Publishing, Paris. DOI: *10.1787/9789264118843-en*

Tyler, T. R. (2001), *Trust and law-abidingness: a proactive model of social regulation*, Centre of Tax System Integrity, The Australian National University, Canberra. *http://regnet.anu.edu.au/sites/default/files/CTSI-WorkingPaper16-full.pdf*

Chapter 4

Tools and guidance for successful implementation

The preceding chapter has established that revenue bodies have substantial experience with Engaging & Involving (E&I) approaches. At the same time it is clear that E&I approaches are increasingly being applied in more systematic, far-reaching, and potentially transformative ways.

This chapter, recognising E&I as a distinct discipline that comes with its own risks and challenges, provides tools and guidance to assist revenue bodies wishing to tap into this potential. The chapter starts by introducing key implementation issues identified through the survey, the workshop and the literature review. The three main themes are then explored in separate sections on capabilities and change management, governance issues, and the challenge of documenting benefits. The chapter concludes with a list summarising key advice emerging out of the chapter.

Key implementation issues

E&I approaches are increasingly being applied in more systematic, far-reaching, and potentially transformative ways. This places more emphasis on E&I as a distinct discipline that, like any other approach, comes with its own risks and challenges that needs to be well considered and managed.

Survey responses and workshop discussions have served to identify perceived enablers and barriers to making progress with mainstreaming E&I approaches. The main factors cited (summarised in Annex C) fall in three broad categories:

- **Building capabilities and managing change:** Lack of capabilities, staff resistance and risk aversion are cited as key barriers to the successful implementation of E&I approaches. Committed management, engaged staff and enabling platforms like frameworks, tools and guidance are on the other hand cited as key success factors.
- **Governing E&I initiatives:** The challenges of approaching SME taxpayers and stakeholders, motivating them to work together, managing expectations and driving E&I processes to a successful end were cited as another barrier.
- **Demonstrating value:** The lack of comprehensive metrics on which to establish the case for E&I approaches constitutes a major barrier. Performance management systems focusing on outputs are ill suited to documenting the benefits of E&I approaches, which will often be working back from the ultimate outcomes.

Revenue bodies further cited the increasingly obvious need for radical innovation to deliver cost reductions and improved performance as an important enabler and driver of change. Lack of resources, lack of will or ability to invest in the longer term, and the costs and complexity of changing legislation, systems and core processes were on the other hand cited as barriers.

This picture reflects experience in other areas of the public sector. The 2011 OECD report *"Together for Better Public Services: Partnering with Citizens and Civil Society"* on co-production practices across the public sector includes reference to an exploratory survey identifying the most frequent barriers to co-production as the most important factors contributing to successful co-production (OECD, 2011a). The most frequent barriers cited are lack of resources, lack of firm evidence, and lack of knowledge and skills as the most frequent barriers to co-production followed by the lack of financial incentives, legal frameworks impeding co-production, and organisational resistance. The most commonly cited success factors are on the other hand: top-level commitment and leadership; willingness and capacity to engage; and clarity of strategy and objectives.

This chapter will on the basis of survey responses, workshop discussions and the literature review explore the three themes outlined above. The tools and guidance offered is intended to assist revenue bodies preparing and implementing E&I initiatives and approaches. The chapter will conclude with a brief list of critical success factors summarising some of the advice.

The chapter, however, makes no claim to exhausting the themes. Instead revenue bodies are encouraged to consult the literature and the additional resources cited in Annex B.

Capabilities and change management

Engaging and involving taxpayers and stakeholders require revenue bodies to work in different ways. This places different demands on revenue body staff, which in many revenue bodies is already being challenged as a result of the broader developments in compliance risk management outlined in Chapter 2. E&I approaches often require revenue body staff to rethink their role as authorities in a context characterised by greater complexity and uncertainty. Revenue body staff may for instance be required to act as facilitators in problem-solving sessions or exploratory processes, which will place demands on communication and negotiation skills, as well as creative thinking, analytic skills and project management.

This has a number of capability-building and change-management implications that came out clearly in survey responses and workshop discussions. The literature similarly identifies capabilities like hard and soft skills, enabling platforms and processes as key success factors for public participation and co-production practices (Bason, 2010). While revenue bodies already engage and involve taxpayers and stakeholders to a large extent, and have varying degrees of experience and capabilities, it would therefore seem reasonable to suggest that revenue bodies looking to harvest the full benefits of E&I approaches can benefit from considerations and investment in this area.

Skills and outsourcing

Revenue bodies have a number of options for building the necessary competences within their respective organisations. They may for instance opt for building central capabilities staffed with specialists hired to provide tailored training for existing staff to build more networked competences within the organisation. Although specialist skills are not required at all levels of the organisation, there will be a need for a degree of understanding and receptiveness throughout the organisation, including among front line staff interacting with taxpayers and stakeholders.

Workshop discussions revealed that revenue bodies are sometimes tempted to outsource E&I processes, although there are few examples of this in practice. However several authors (for instance OECD, 2011; Bason, 2010) points out that commissioning is also a specialist skill. Bason further cautions: "What is crucial, though, is to *never* subcontract the entire process to someone outside the organisation, depositing key experiences, insights and learning to people who will never have to live with the outcomes of the process. There should be a very hands-on, engaged and proactive nature to the way the public organisation's own staff are involved, and there must be clear accountability and engagement at leadership level, ensuring access to the relevant hierarchies and an ongoing connection to other activities and innovation processes in the organisation." (Bason, 2010: 210).

The risk related to outsourcing, in short, is that rather than becoming an integrated part of organisational practices and culture, E&I approaches may be perceived as an add-on to be delivered by external consultants. This will not have the same impact on the organisation, which also will not acquire the experience and expertise necessary for building momentum for further change. This does not mean, however, that outsourcing cannot be the right choice, but only that it needs to be considered in the bigger context of capability building and change management. In this context Bason suggests looking for the middle ground: often combination of in-house innovation experts and some external support can work well (Bason, 2010).

Mind-set and organisational culture

Survey responses and workshop discussions also identified mind-set and organisational culture as key factors influencing the success of E&I approaches. These factors complement skills and capabilities, but there also is a degree of overlap, as a change in skills and capabilities will also impact on mind-set and culture. Mind-set and culture may at the same time be a barrier and an enabler, although workshop discussions suggest that it is frequently experienced as a barrier. At the same time change can sometimes be met with resistance and cynicism in large organisations, especially if it challenges or is perceived to challenge established hierarchies and interests.

During the workshop, a group discussed how revenue bodies might organise themselves to develop a stronger user-orientation and stimulate innovation. The group defined an ideal scenario to determine what changes were needed. The ideal scenario defined by the group involved end-users being at the centre of revenue body strategies and activities; staff with diverse skills and professional backgrounds being willing to experiment and learn; and revenue body performance being evaluated in terms of outcomes rather than outputs. The group suggested that working back from such a scenario might be a useful methodology to develop a roadmap for change.

The literature establishes that E&I approaches are enhanced by organisational cultures receptive to different professional approaches, outside views and new forms of working (OECD, 2011a). One researcher observes with reference to tax administration that it is counterproductive to see clients as crooks; instead it is desirable that client focus be a permanent and pervasive part of organisational culture (Alford, 2009).

These observations suggest that dedicated change management efforts are required to harvest the full benefits of E&I approaches. E&I approaches themselves may contribute to bringing about this change by bringing in the views and perspectives of taxpayers and stakeholders into the organisation and challenging dominant views. The gradual accumulation of experience and evidence also contributes to overcoming resistance and building momentum for change. It would be consistent with the principles underlying E&I approaches to consider opportunities to involve internal and perhaps even external stakeholders in designing new strategies and practices.

It was observed at the workshop that the testimonies of taxpayers and stakeholders can be a powerful catalyst for change. This is reflected in the literature. Bason points out that undigested representations of client experience can be an eye-opener generating the "professional empathy" allowing staff to connect or reconnect to the reality of the clients they serve (Bason, 2010). The example at the opening of Chapter 2 illustrates the dramatic impact testimonies reflecting user experience can have even at the highest level in a revenue body.

Enabling platforms and incentives

A discussion of capabilities and change management would not be complete without considering enabling platforms and incentives. Survey responses and workshop discussions suggest that E&I approaches are enhanced by enabling platforms like central capabilities, methodologies and guidelines to support practice. Some observers similarly point out that it is desirable to align strategies, capabilities and key organisational processes to make sure they properly support E&I approaches (Coats & Passmore, 2008). In this context, revenue bodies may benefit from developing frameworks underscoring commitment and clarifying how E&I approaches relate to wider organisational strategies, as discussed in Chapter 3. A well-established international standard for stakeholder engagement may also provide inspiration in this regard – see Box 4.1.

Box 4.1 AccountAbility Stakeholder Engagement Standard

The global consultancy in standards for sustainability and responsibility, AccountAbility, has developed a *Stakeholder Engagement Standard* to help organisations ensure that engagement processes are purpose driven, robust and deliver results.

The standard offers a principles-based, open source framework for quality stakeholder engagement:

- **Commitment and integration:** The standard requires that formal commitment to stakeholder engagement is made, that stakeholder engagement is integrated into relevant governance and decision-making processes, and that stakeholder engagement is used systematically and regularly in ways affecting both strategy and operations.
- **Purpose, scope and stakeholders:** The standard further requires that clarity is established around purpose and scope of stakeholder engagement, and that decisions about what stakeholders to engage are based on thorough stakeholder mapping.
- **Stakeholder engagement process:** The standard finally requires that a quality stakeholder engagement process comprising the full project cycle (plan, prepare, implement, and review) is designed and implemented, and that stakeholders are engaged in all phases of this process.

The standard (which can be used as a stand-alone standard or integrated with other standards) is supported by detailed practical guidance supporting these principles, including step-by-step guidance for each of the four phases in the project cycle. A two volume stakeholder engagement manual is also available.

More information is available at: *www.accountability.org*

To stimulate change, innovative behaviour must also be recognised and rewarded. As discussed in the section on documenting benefits, performance metrics often reflects outputs rather than outcomes. Similarly at the area or individual level, organisations often measure and reward performance in terms that do not necessarily reflect the contribution to meeting the ultimate objectives of the organisation. Discussions at the workshop suggested that it is necessary to build innovation incentives into metrics and reward structures. Alongside these material incentives to innovation, revenue bodies may also consider symbolic incentives in the form of awards and public recognition. Finally it is, as one workshop participant observed, in itself an important incentive that ideas are taken seriously.

Management buy-in

Finally sponsorship at the top level in organisations was frequently referred to in survey responses and workshop discussions as the single most important success factor. This is reflected in the literature. Bason, for instance, observes on the basis of substantial experience with E&I approaches in the public sector: "In my experience, only where a responsible manager has 'got it' and really embraced the co-creation process is it likely that benefit will be harvested. 'Getting it' includes facing the pain of *really* seeing what doesn't work today, and having the courage to embrace divergence, envisaging how different the future could be, and motivating the staff to stick to the process, even if the findings may be unpleasant." (Bason, 2010: 211).

Management need to be committed to E&I approaches not only in order for investments to be made and incentives to be put in place, but also for a range of other reasons. The commitment at the top level is critical in a change management perspective.

E&I approaches are also likely to generate insights meriting the attention of management, as they have implications for strategies, processes and systems, as illustrated by the review of experience in Chapter 3. Finally management need to be able to explain and defend E&I approaches to internal and external stakeholders, and to see the occasional failure in the wider strategic context where E&I approaches is an important driver of innovation and leverage.

The workshop identified driving testimonies reflecting the experience of taxpayers and stakeholders to the top of the organisation as a powerful strategy for creating commitment to change.

Governing initiatives

Survey responses and workshop discussions revealed that revenue bodies experience a range of challenges relating to the governance of E&I initiatives. This section will briefly discuss these challenges and offer some strategies for addressing them based on advice offered by revenue bodies or in literature. The section will start with approaching methodologies and engagement processes at the high level and then proceed to discuss more practical aspects of deciding with whom to engage and managing stakeholder relationships.

Methodologies and engagement processes

While revenue bodies already engage and involve taxpayers and stakeholders in a variety of ways, it is clear that more systematic and far-reaching approaches is new territory for most revenue bodies. This means that they are presented with a number of practical challenges like deciding when and with whom to engage, what approaches to apply, how to prepare for the engagement, how to carry out the engagement, and how to evaluate the engagement.

Robust methodologies and clearly defined engagement processes can help manage this complexity. This is illustrated by an example from New Zealand, where Inland Revenue, building on the stakeholder engagement standard referenced earlier in this chapter, has developed a "stakeholder engagement toolkit" combining clearly defined processes with more hands-on guidance and tools – see Box 4.2.

The literature similarly offers some advice. Wilcox (Wilcox, 1994) suggests that it is helpful to think of participation in four phases: the initiation phase in which interest is triggered, the preparation phase, the participation phase in which engagement take place, and the continuation phase where commitment is reaffirmed. Naturally there is also the option of discontinuation if a relationship is dysfunctional or fails to deliver the desired results. Revenue bodies need to periodically review relationships to determine in which relationships to invest.

Box 4.2 Stakeholder Engagement Toolkit in New Zealand

Inland Revenue in New Zealand has developed a "stakeholder engagement toolkit" to support implementation. The toolkit offers a five-step methodology as well as a range of tools and templates to help staff and managers plan, manage and evaluate engagement initiatives.

The five phases of the methodology are:

- **Defining the purpose of the engagement:** The first step of the methodology is to define the purposes of the engagement and to consider scope, accountabilities and other issues.
- **Identifying and analysing stakeholders:** The second step is to identify taxpayers and stakeholders that could potentially be engaged, analyse their interests and the possible contributions they can make to the objective, consider the current relationship, and to prioritise with whom to engage.
- **Designing tactical engagement:** The third step is the preparation of the actual engagement. This involves a review of staff capabilities (in areas like communication, technical skills and relationship management) and the preparation of stakeholder engagement plans considering purpose and scope of engagement; stakeholder interests, resources and current relationship; issues, risks and opportunities; success measures; and communications.
- **Undertaking engagement:** The fourth step is the actual engagement. This involves approaching the stakeholders, managing the relationship, and keeping track of progress and the engagement history.
- **Evaluating effectiveness:** The final step is evaluating the effectiveness of the engagement. This involves seeking feedback from stakeholders and staff involved with a view to identifying opportunities for improvement.

The different steps are supported by a range of tools and templates to support practice. For instance, stakeholder identification and analysis is supported by an engagement continuum showing the current versus desired status of the relationship on a five-phase continuum: co-exist, network, cooperate, collaborate and partner. The actual engagement phase is also supported by a set of principles to support staff in interacting with stakeholders. The principles focus on professional behaviour, inclusion and integrity.

Inland Revenue finds that the stakeholder engagement toolkit is a helpful framework for supporting staff and managers involved in E&I activities. It is recognised, however, that one size does not fit all purposes and relationships and that a degree of flexibility is required to be able to adapt to the needs of particular circumstances.

Deciding with whom to engage

A first step is deciding whom to engage. Alford (Alford, 2009) suggest drawing a web of causality in order to identify key points and actors to be influenced. Here revenue bodies may benefit from standardised templates for drawing causality-webs or stakeholder maps. A tool like the engagement continuum used in New Zealand may also be helpful for framing the discussion about how to develop relationships with key stakeholders identified through this exercise.

Alford also have some practical considerations about whom to involve. In his view it is wasteful to have specialised tasks performed by clients and stakeholders, especially if these are experts in something else. Instead he suggests that collaborative approaches are appropriate in two scenarios: where the unique contribution of clients and stakeholders is required and where clients and stakeholders are more able to perform the task.

Another aspect of deciding with whom to engage is representativeness. This theme came out strongly in survey responses and workshop discussions and is also reflected in the literature. Revenue bodies naturally need to consider when representativeness is needed and how it can in these cases be achieved. The focus on representativeness as a technical discipline relying on statistical sampling and similar methods can, however, be misleading. Revenue bodies need to think at a more fundamental level about what it means to engage and involve different groups, what assumptions are driving these choices, and what the methodological and other implications are.

A number of observations can be made in this regard:

- SME industry organisations have their own legitimate interests and are not necessarily representative of SME views and perspectives. In some respects they do not know SMEs better than the revenue body do. For some purposes it can therefore be desirable or even necessary to go directly to the SMEs themselves.
- E&I processes may become "hijacked" by particularly articulate stakeholders lobbying for their own interests while less articulate groups are left out or not adequately represented. It can therefore be necessary to devise processes to make sure that the results are not overly biased by the views and interests of expert lobbyists at the expense of less organised and articulate groups.
- Taxpayers and stakeholders may for a variety of reasons feel compelled to provide "strategic" answers to questions from the revenue body in the context of consultation or social research. It can therefore be necessary to think about more open-ended forms of research to develop more accurate representations of their views and interests.
- E&I processes may involve a risk of "institutionalising" certain groups or segments who gradually become expert users trained in revenue body discourse. This may particularly be an issue with long-standing relationships and with frequent engagement of the same taxpayers or stakeholders. This overreliance on particular groups or segments may also lead to engagement or survey fatigue, which should be thought of as a potential cost.

The issue is thus more about critical awareness than about representativeness as such. Sometimes "innovating from the extremes" may even be a deliberate strategy. This in a sense is the idea in lead user methodologies. Revenue bodies may also think about involving subsets of the population that face particular challenges with the way the tax system is designed and operated. This may be particular ethnic or social groups. It could also be people who for different reasons feel uneasy about technologies, authorities, forms or bureaucratic jargon. Improving the tax system for these groups could likely lead to improvements for the population as a whole.

Key aspects of relationship management

A first step in establishing a relationship is approaching the taxpayers or stakeholders to be engaged. Survey responses and workshop discussions indicate that revenue bodies often feel somewhat uneasy about this step. A useful starting point is, in the experience of one revenue body, to find a shared agenda that goes beyond compliance. This can be facilitated by approaching the problem in a broader perspective rather than through the lens of the revenue body. Therefore it can be helpful to engage and involve taxpayers and stakeholders at an early stage when the problem is still being explored.

As indicated in the discussion of the benefits of E&I approaches in Chapter 2, there is a range of shared or at least compatible interests that allow for win-win situations to be identified and explored.

Mutual trust is central to a successful relationship. Trust is gradually established as parties develop experience with each other over time. Revenue bodies as an authority vested with coercive powers often start from a low point in this process. Some revenue bodies indicate that taxpayers and stakeholders sometimes express doubt as to whether the revenue body genuinely value their feedback or is sincere in its intent to engage in more collaborative approaches. This is, however, also an opportunity, as taxpayers and stakeholders may be positively surprised, as their assumptions about the revenue body are challenged by a different behaviour. To establish a circle of virtue where trust is gradually enhanced, it is important to be genuine and consistent.

Revenue body experience suggests that it can be helpful to create a safe setting – especially when dealing with controversial topics. It can further facilitate relationship building to have clearly defined ground rules. In Australia engagement often take place in forums governed by a charter outlining purpose and protocols. In some cases it can make sense to outsource activities like interviews on delicate subjects to a third party.

A closely related issue is managing expectations, as the failure to properly manage expectations can lead to the erosion of trust and damage relationships. Survey responses indicated that taxpayers and stakeholders often expect faster and more spectacular results than are feasible. Sometimes they may wish to discuss issues outside the scope of the conversation or outside the reach of the revenue body, including (in the experience of one revenue body) the tax rates themselves. Taxpayers and stakeholders may also be reluctant to accept situations when their views or ideas cannot be accommodated – especially as they do not always appreciate the complexity and constraints of the bigger legal, administrative and political context in which the revenue body is operating.

Workshop discussions suggested a range of strategies for managing expectations. These strategies can be summarised in this three step approach, although they will of course have to be adapted to particular needs and circumstances:

- **Defining scope and boundaries up front:** First, it was considered critical to define scope and boundaries up front and make sure that they are understood and accepted by all parties. Acceptance and ownership by taxpayers and stakeholders can in this context be enhanced by defining scope and boundaries through dialogue.
- **Discussing process and progress:** Second, it was considered important to discuss the process with taxpayers and stakeholders and provide feedback on progress. Transparency around process requirements and challenges faced will also help taxpayers and stakeholders understand why pragmatic choices sometimes need to be made.
- **Providing feedback:** Finally, it was considered important to provide taxpayers and stakeholders with feedback. This should ideally include acknowledgement of their contribution, explanation of why some suggestions were modified or not taken on board, and indication of what will happen next.

An important part of managing expectations is acknowledging the role of the revenue body as an authority. Revenue bodies, however sincere in their intent to involve taxpayers and stakeholders, need to balance the horizontal nature of E&I relationships with the, by definition, more vertical nature of the regulator-subject relationship without compromising either. Being clear about the role as authority will help taxpayers and stakeholders understand why different concerns will sometimes need to be balanced. It will also enhance accountability and help ensure that the revenue body is not perceived to give preferential treatment to particular stakeholders.

A final consideration is that trust and understanding will often depend on the relationships between individuals, which may threaten continuity when these individuals change positions. This goes both ways. Several revenue bodies indicate that they have experienced relationships suffering when key staff with industry bodies or other stakeholders have changed positions. It is thus important to make sure that both sides think about institutionalising relationships and ensuring continuity.

Demonstrating the benefits

A recurring theme in survey responses and workshop discussions has been the need to demonstrate the benefits of engaging and involving taxpayers and stakeholders. Many revenue bodies have brought up the question of how to quantify value and establish business cases for particular initiatives. A related question has been, noting that only a limited evidence base is available, how to make the case for the approach in the absence of conclusive evidence. This section will address some key issues related to demonstrating the benefits of E&I approaches.

The review of current and emerging practices in the previous chapter led to the observation that there are few examples of approaches with robust evaluation setups. It is, however, important to note that the need to demonstrate value or the inherent challenges in doing so is by no means unique to E&I approaches, but applies to all approaches. The absence of conclusive evidence seems to function much more as a *barrier* to the adoption of innovative approaches than as a *push factor* away from more mainstreamed approaches. Viewed in terms of outcomes, traditional approaches are not supported by a solid evidence base, even if they perform well in terms of narrow output measures.

Any discussion on demonstrating benefits needs to be firmly rooted in the wider discussion on public value. It was established in Chapter 2 that E&I approaches are closely related to a shift in perspective about what constitutes public value. An important element of this is the tendency for revenue bodies and other public agencies to define their purpose and evaluate their performance in terms of outcomes rather than outputs. Many of the benefits of E&I approaches relate to improved outcomes, although it is acknowledged that they can also contribute to cheaper and better outputs, and the challenge is therefore to a large extent about demonstrating these improved outcomes.

The emphasis on outcomes involves a focus on the actual value public agencies are intended to deliver, which in itself can contribute significantly to innovation and improved performance (Bason, 2010). At the same time a shift to outcomes involves a number of challenges when it comes to measurement and evaluation. While outputs (like number of audits or audit yield) are relatively straightforward to measure, it is more difficult to measure outcomes and attribute these to revenue body activities. This challenge is naturally particularly pronounced for sophisticated interventions where a number of components interact, as will often be the case for E&I approaches.

Recognising these challenges, the FTA has produced a guidance note to assist revenue bodies in evaluating the effectiveness of compliance risk treatment strategies – see Box 4.3. The note offers in-depth discussion of issues related to outcome evaluation, a methodology for evaluating the effectiveness of compliance risk treatment strategies, and examples of evaluation designs applied by revenue bodies. It is accompanied by a suite of products offering an overview of the main methodologies available.

Some of the advice from the guidance note and the accompanying material was echoed in workshop discussions. In particular it was suggested to design activities around intended outcomes and think about evaluation from the beginning. It was further recommended to be explicit about the underlying programme theory, how this is supported by evidence and what assumptions are made. Finally there was consensus that there is a need to be pragmatic about evaluation. While robust evaluation setups may be required for high-profiled initiatives, more pragmatic approaches may suffice for other initiatives. One specific suggestion was relying on a sensitivity analysis to make a convincing case for innovative approaches where no firm evidence is available.

Box 4.3 Evaluating the effectiveness of compliance risk treatment strategies

Revenue bodies have a responsibility to use their limited resources in the most cost-effective manner and to be accountable about the extent to which activities contribute to achieving agreed objectives.

The 2010 guidance note *Evaluating the Effectiveness of Compliance Risk Treatment Strategies* sets out a practical methodology for conducting outcome evaluations of compliance risk treatment strategies in priority areas. It draws on innovative work, based on considerable research, carried out by one OECD revenue body, and considerable further assistance from a number of other revenue bodies that have been intensifying their efforts to better understand the impacts/effectiveness of their compliance activities.

After outlining a number of important concepts and issues often raised in an evaluation context (including the output/outcome distinction, programme logic, and attribution), the guidance note introduces and elaborates on a four phase compliance effectiveness methodology:

- understanding and articulating the risk;
- expressing desired outcomes and identifying the right mix of strategies in order to target causes rather than symptoms;
- identifying potential indicators for each compliance strategy and validating them to ensure they are viable and useful; and
- evaluating and reporting on the extent to which a revenue body has been effective in achieving these outcomes over the immediate, intermediate and long term.

The guidance note gives emphasis to the identification and development of practical measures and indicators that, set at the commencement of risk treatment action, can be used to gauge progress and assess the merits of risk treatment strategies in terms of improved taxpayer compliance and confidence in a revenue body's administration. To illustrate these aspects, the note includes a large number of case study examples from a cross-section of revenue bodies, describing specific measures and indicators used to evaluate the impacts of specific risk treatments and, for most, the impacts observed.

The note acknowledges that for some strategies there are limitations as to degree of precision/confidence that can be attached to conclusions concerning their impacts and effectiveness. The note also acknowledges that it is not possible, nor even desirable, for a revenue body to fully evaluate every specific risk treatment carried out, given the burden this would present.

The guidance note is accompanied by a *briefing document* for senior decision makers, a *background note* on revenue body and public sector experience, and a *compendium* providing detailed information on some of the methodologies available.

The full suite of products is available at the FTA website: *www.oecd.org/tax/fta*

A discussion on documenting the benefits would not be complete without also considering some aspects that are particular to the approach. Engaging and involving taxpayers and stakeholders involves drawing on their time, goodwill and trust, which in turn is justified by what they achieve, including the experience of participation itself. This raises questions about assessing (or at least estimating) external costs, documenting external benefits, and evaluating the quality of the participation. It would seem coherent with the principles underlying the approach to consider ways in which taxpayers and stakeholders could be involved in evaluating these aspects.

A final observation from the literature is that innovative approaches call for more innovative performance accounts (Bason, 2010). This could be in the form of performance accounts drawing on qualitative data and contrasting narratives emerging out of this with the underlying programme theory to assess to what extent this confirms or challenges the rationale for the intervention. In this way a focus on taxpayers and stakeholders challenges revenue bodies not only to operate in new ways, but also to reconsider how performance is measured and evaluated.

Key advice for implementation

This chapter has discussed key implementation challenges identified in the survey and workshop discussions and reflected in the literature. Based on the themes discussed, it is possible to draw up a list summarising some of the advice – see Box 4.4. While the list makes no claim to being exhaustive, it provides revenue bodies with a useful summary of key advice to support implementation.

Box 4.4 Key advice for implementation

Start with what you have: Revenue bodies are already using E&I approaches in a variety of ways. To make further progress, it is advisable to build on the existing resources and capabilities, but think about scaling as opportunities arise and as the case for E&I approaches gradually become more firmly established and accepted. As with other new approaches, "think big, start small".

Be genuine and consistent: Revenue bodies sometimes face skepticism about the sincerity of their desire to engage and involve taxpayers and stakeholders. Trust and legitimacy is enhanced as this skepticism is gradually overcome. The opposite may happen, however, if the revenue body is perceived to not be sincere or to hold hidden agendas. It is therefore critical that E&I processes always be genuine.

Be open and flexible: Engaging and involving taxpayers and stakeholders involves an element of unpredictability, as their views and perspectives will often challenge revenue body assumptions and interrupt traditional linear processes. It is therefore important to be sufficiently open and flexible to pick up and act upon these new insights, which will often lead to better outcomes and solutions.

Avoid overpromising and under-delivering: E&I approaches can sometimes generate expectations among taxpayers and stakeholders that can be difficult to meet. It is therefore important to carefully manage expectations by being clear on purpose, trade-offs and limitations. In particular, revenue bodies should avoid overpromising and under-delivering, as this may backfire on credibility.

Celebrate successes and learn from failures: The benefits of a successful E&I initiative can often be intuitively understood. Celebrate successes to anchor learning generate further momentum for change. Accept, on the other hand, that innovative approaches sometimes involve a degree of calculated risk-taking and embrace the occasional failure as a learning opportunity.

Be patient and persistent: Revenue bodies may identify some quick wins, but as with other new approaches, it is necessary to "sow before harvesting". Commitment and investment is required to develop capabilities and manage change. Building trust and developing relationships with external stakeholders also takes time and effort. A long-term perspective is therefore important.

Work back from outcomes: Performance metrics and incentive structures relying excessively on outputs is a key barrier to the take-up of innovative approaches. Working back from desired outcomes can, on the other hand, stimulate innovation and change. Consider how your organisation can benefit from focusing on its ultimate outcomes and how this can be reflected in metrics and incentives.

Bibliography

AccountAbility.org (1999), *AA1000 Stakeholder Engagement Standard (AA1000SES).* *www.accountability.org/images/content/5/4/542/AA1000SES%202010%20PRINT.pdf*

Alford, J. (2009), *Engaging Public Sector Clients: From Service-Delivery to Co-Production*, Palgrave Macmillan and Houndmills, New York.

Bason, C. (2010), *Leading Public Sector Innovation: Co-creating for a Better Society*, Policy Press, Bristol.

Coats, D. & E. Passmore (2008), *Public Value: The Next Steps in Public Service Reform*, Work Foundation, London. *www.theworkfoundation.com/assets/docs/publications/201_PV_public_service_reform_final.pdf*

OECD (2011a), *Together for Better Public Services: Partnering with Citizens and Civil Society*, OECD Public Governance Reviews, OECD Publishing, Paris. DOI: *10.1787/9789264118843-en*

OECD (2010b), *Evaluating the Effectiveness of Compliance Risk Treatment Strategies*, Forum on Tax Administration, OECD, Paris. *www.oecd.org/document/31/0,3746,en_2649_33749_46282143_1_1_1_1,00.html*

Wilcox, D. (1994), *The Guide to Effective Participation*, open source participation guide. *www.partnerships.org.uk/guide/index.htm*

Chapter 5

Findings and recommendations

Engaging and involving taxpayers and stakeholders offer the opportunity to mobilise knowledge and resources residing outside the revenue body. This can contribute significantly to improved outcomes, cost reductions and a range of other benefits. It can also enhance the legitimacy of the tax system and trust in the revenue body, which are crucial factors for voluntary compliance.

The preceding chapters have provided an introduction to the Engaging & Involving (E&I) concept, a stock take of current and emerging practices, and guidance for successful implementation. This chapter will bring out key findings from previous chapters and set out recommendations to assist revenue bodies make further progress.

This report has explored how engaging and involving taxpayers and stakeholders can contribute to a range of benefits to revenue bodies, taxpayers, stakeholders, and society at large. In the current economic climate revenue bodies are under pressure to do more with less. At the same time, creating the conditions for growth is a central policy priority, which gives renewed emphasis on the importance of promoting a level playing field and reducing the administrative burden falling on businesses. By engaging and involving taxpayers and stakeholders, revenue bodies can explore these mutual or compatible interests to deliver more value for money.

The relevance of E&I approaches is, however, not limited to the present economic climate. Engaging and involving citizens in the design and delivery of public services has been a major trend across the public sector in many countries in the last decade. The trend is linked to a changing understanding of the nature of the problems the public sector is facing and a changing vision of what constitutes public value. It is increasingly recognised that many of the problems faced by the public sector – even the less "wicked" ones – cannot be effectively resolved by top-down approaches implemented by single agencies. It is also increasingly recognised that what ultimately matters is not the output of services and regulatory efforts, but the extent to which these activities contribute to the desired outcomes like health, safety and a clean environment. Here the input of citizens can contribute to improving solutions, providing public agencies with leverage in the actual delivery, and sometimes even substitute public sector input. At the same time, engaging and involving citizens can enhance trust, accountability and democratic governance.

Not surprisingly, these developments also have parallels in tax administration. Recent work by the FTA show how revenue bodies increasingly are adopting an outcome focus and shifting attention to the compliance environment in which outcomes are shaped by a range of factors not easily influenced by traditional approaches. As a consequence, revenue bodies are seeking to shift activities *upwards* in the value stream through preventive measures or lasting changes to the compliance environment, and *outwards* through increased collaboration with taxpayers and stakeholders. These themes came out strongly in the *"Right from the start: influencing the compliance environment for SMEs"* information note, which contains a number of examples showing how engaging and involving taxpayers and stakeholders can enhance the management of compliance risks for the SME segment. They have also found expression in the large business area, where the relationship between taxpayers and the revenue body has been altered by "enhanced relationship" or "cooperative compliance" arrangements providing a platform for upfront resolution of risks and issues.

E&I approaches offer substantial benefits to revenue bodies. By engaging and involving taxpayers and stakeholders, revenue bodies can improve their understanding of risks and issues, key explanatory factors, and appropriate solutions. They can also benefit from the involvement of taxpayers and stakeholders in the design, implementation and evaluation of these solutions. Engaging and involving taxpayers and stakeholders can for instance enhance the identification of risks, contribute to more tailored service offerings or compliance interventions, and help revenue bodies achieve greater reach through one-to-many approaches leveraged by stakeholders, technologies and media. It can also help identify opportunities to eliminate sources of error, design more meaningful and efficient processes, or improve the functioning of the tax system in other ways. This can in turn contribute significantly to improved outcomes, cost reductions, and improved service experience. It can also be part of a virtuous circle, as trust and confidence in the tax system and the revenue body is strongly correlated to voluntary compliance.

At the same time, engaging and involving taxpayers and stakeholders offers substantial external benefits. E&I approaches can for instance contribute to promoting a level playing field and help reducing the administrative burden, which are key priorities for (compliant) SMEs and their representative bodies. They can also contribute to smoother processes and improved service experience beyond what is captured by reference to the administrative burden. And for some stakeholders (like intermediaries) collaborating with the revenue body may foster innovation, help consolidate their position or lead to new business opportunities. These benefits, in addition to any material compensation offered, are crucial in creating the win-win situations motivating the contribution of taxpayers and stakeholders. Moreover, taxpayers and stakeholders will often contribute simply because they identify with the purposes of the revenue body.

The stock take of current and emerging practices in this report show that revenue bodies have substantial experience with E&I approaches. A number of revenue bodies have made formal commitments to engaging and involving taxpayers and stakeholders, and others are working on more systematic approaches or are building specialist capabilities. In most countries, taxpayers and stakeholders are consulted about major changes to the tax system and its administration, and revenue bodies often play a key role in these processes. Most revenue bodies also have fairly consolidated mechanisms for consultation and collaboration with SME industry bodies and intermediaries, and in some cases these have evolved into lasting partnerships. In addition, a host of E&I activities take place across the different categories of compliance activities:

- **Information and guidance:** E&I approaches seem most mainstreamed for information and guidance. Most revenue bodies are taking advantage of social research or user-testing methodologies to tailor the services offered to the needs and expectations of taxpayers and stakeholders, and some have established design labs or similar capabilities for user-testing or user-driven innovation. Many revenue bodies are also actively collaborating with stakeholders like intermediaries and SME industry bodies to design or deliver these services, and in some cases formal partnerships have been established.
- **Compliance risk management:** Revenue bodies engage and involve taxpayers and stakeholders to some extent during all phases of the risk management cycle. This is not least true as far as improving the understanding of the risks, tailoring interventions, or seeking leverage for the interventions is concerned. Involving taxpayers and stakeholders in risk identification and prioritisation, treatment design, and evaluation is less common, although this would appear meaningful in the context of partnership-based approaches.
- **Systemic solutions:** Revenue bodies increasingly engage and involve taxpayers and stakeholders in the context of systemic solutions. It is widely acknowledged that systemic solutions are often enhanced or made possible by the participation of taxpayers and stakeholders. Examples range from consultation on changes to forms and processes over collaboration on digital interfaces or systems integration to formal partnerships on standards for accounting solutions and POS systems.

Individual SME taxpayers are generally engaged more on an ad hoc basis whereas stakeholders are more often involved in more lasting and deeper forms of collaboration. Revenue bodies have most experience working with intermediaries and industry bodies. There are also good examples of collaboration with stakeholders in the SME compliance chain (notably developers and vendors of accounting solutions and POS systems) on systemic solutions and SME industry partners (principal contractors) on compliance risk management initiatives, although these practices are not mainstreamed. Finally there would seem to be significant potential for further collaboration with SME business partners, civil society, and (paradoxically) other government bodies.

The focus for collaboration depends on the particular stakeholder, the risk or issue addressed, and the specific circumstances. Often the collaboration will be a component of a broader initiative with one or more leverage strategies reinforcing each other. For instance revenue bodies may seek to leverage on the knowledge, reach, credibility and efforts of stakeholders or on intelligence, technology, social norms and media. Collaboration tends to deepen when the object for improvement is (in whole or in part) external to the revenue body, as will often be the case when working with systemic solutions. Experience further indicates that E&I approaches work best and add most value when the perspectives of taxpayers and stakeholders are brought in from the beginning of the process or at a sufficiently early stage to allow their contributions to influence the framing and understanding of the problem and the search for solutions.

While the rationale for these strategies is clear, and the overall experience encouraging, few examples include robust evaluation setups allowing for benefits to be firmly established. Most examples are instead underpinned by plausible (if implicit) assumptions and their impact illustrated with reference to improved outputs (for instance a simplified procedure or an improved product) or positive feedback. There would therefore seem to be significant potential for further developing or articulating the underlying programme theory, linking it to reliable indicators allowing for the tracking of outcomes, and quantifying the benefits by sensitivity analysis and other means.

Against this background, revenue bodies are encouraged to:

- **Assess their current experience and consider opportunities for more systematic and far-reaching approaches:** The collective experience with E&I approaches documented in this report is sufficiently broad and deep that there should be something to inspire everybody. Revenue bodies that already have mainstreamed E&I approaches in some areas may benefit from applying more systematic approaches or from developing more far-reaching and potentially transformative initiatives.

- **Assess their current capabilities and consider opportunities for better supporting the mainstreaming of E&I approaches:** E&I is increasingly recognised as a distinct approach requiring specialist capabilities not just in terms of competences, but also in terms of organisational culture, values and mind-set. This may in turn affect HRM practices (in areas like recruitment, training, remuneration and reward systems) and organisational structure. Revenue bodies may benefit from considering these issues in the context of their wider strategies and capability-building efforts.

- **Assess how E&I approaches fit with their current performance evaluation framework and consider opportunities for strengthening the outcome focus:** Narrow output measures are relatively easy to work with, but may channel attention and resources away from innovative approaches. Documenting outcomes and attributing them to revenue body activities (and their individual components) on the other hand represents a number of challenges. Therefore more pragmatic approaches are often required. Revenue bodies may find inspiration in previous work of the FTA.

Annex A. Survey form

Part 1. General information

Respondent identification

Respondent name and contact details	

Framework for engaging and involving taxpayers and stakeholders

A systematic emphasis on engaging and involving taxpayers and stakeholders may have implications for the management and public profile of the revenue body.

How and to what extent is the approach reflected in the following areas?

High level strategic statements and documents *What are the key messages relating to engaging and involving taxpayers and stakeholders in high level strategic statements and documents?*	
Annual plans and reports *What messages and other content around engaging and involving taxpayers and stakeholders are included in annual plans and reports?*	
Other external communication *How are intentions for engaging and involving taxpayers and stakeholders reflected in other external communication?*	

Practices of engaging and involving taxpayers and stakeholders

Public consultation

Most revenue bodies have a practice of consulting with stakeholders and/or the general public on significant changes to the tax system and its administration.

Does your revenue body have such a practice? And if so: what do you do to ensure that the views of SMEs are represented?

Forums

Many revenue bodies have put in place specific forums as mechanisms for engaging and involving taxpayers and stakeholders. Examples are forums for the accountancy profession and forums for SME industry organisations.

What forums (or similar mechanisms for engaging and involving SME taxpayers and stakeholders) exist in your country? What is the nature and extent of the engagement and involvement? And what has resulted from it?

The accountancy profession	
SME industry organisations	
Others	

Engaging and involving taxpayers and stakeholders in compliance activities

Recent work by the sub-group has revealed that revenue bodies increasingly engage and involve SME taxpayers and stakeholders as part of their efforts to enhance compliance. This engagement and involvement may in principle happen in the context of any activity undertaken to enhance compliance. It can also take many forms ranging from basic consultation over various forms of co-operation to more complex forms of co-production.

The different forms of engaging and involving taxpayers and stakeholders can be illustrated by the preliminary continuum model (subject to further refinement) below:

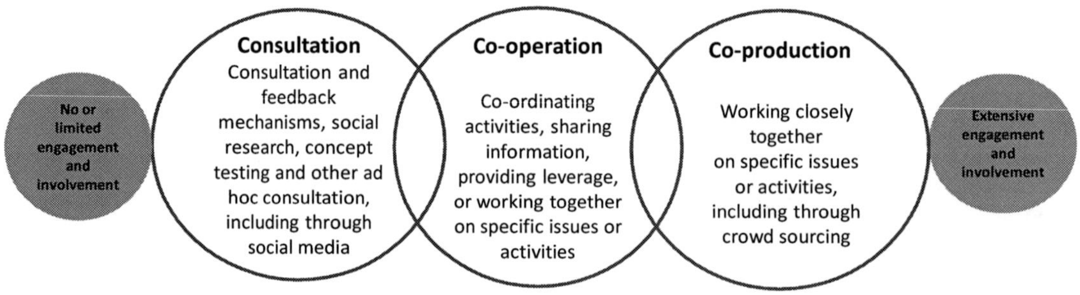

How and to what extent does your revenue body engage and involve SME taxpayers and stakeholders in the following areas? (Please provide general information for each category, but think at the same time of specific examples, preferably from the co-operation and co-production categories, that can be further detailed using the template in Part 2 of this survey form).

Information and guidance Involving SME taxpayers and stakeholders in the design and delivery of information and guidance may contribute to better products and outcomes. *How and to what extent does your revenue body involve SME taxpayers and stakeholders in the design and delivery of information and guidance?*	

Risk management activities Revenue bodies may (at least in principle) involve taxpayers and stakeholders in all stages of the compliance risk management process, including identification and prioritisation of risks, design and implementation of treatments, and evaluation. Leveraging the resources of SME taxpayers and stakeholders may contribute to improved compliance outcomes and generate other benefits. *How and to what extent does your revenue body involve SME taxpayers and stakeholders in compliance risk management activities?*	
Systemic solutions Revenue bodies share an interest with compliant SME taxpayers and stakeholders in nurturing an environment that is favourable to compliance. This may for instance be done by working with taxpayers and stakeholders to simplify and improve systems, procedures, forms, interfaces and control chains. *How and to what extent does your revenue body involve SME taxpayers and stakeholders in activities designed to improve aspects of the compliance environment, including by taking advantage of opportunities offered by new technologies?*	

Please use the attached template (Part 2) to provide specific examples of implemented or planned initiatives.

Overall experience

It would be helpful if you could elaborate a bit on your overall experience with engaging and involving taxpayers and stakeholders.

Benefits for revenue body *What are the benefits for the revenue body of engaging and involving taxpayers and stakeholders? To what extent have you been able to quantify these benefits?*	
Incentives for taxpayers and stakeholders *What are the incentives for taxpayers and stakeholders to work more closely with the revenue body? How effective do these incentives appear to be in practice?*	
Challenges *What are the main challenges involved? And what strategies seem most appropriate for overcoming these?*	

Suggestions for workshop

A project workshop is planned to take place in Oslo on 8-10 October.

Do you have suggestions for themes and issues that should be given particular attention at the project workshop?

Expected contribution of report

It will be helpful to know your expectations for the final output of the project.

What do you expect from the project report? What would be a good contribution? And do you have any specific suggestions for themes or issues that could be covered?

References to research and other relevant material

A horizon scan will be carried out to identify research and other material that can add value to the project. This may for instance be material providing leverage in establishing the case for engaging and involving the public, experience from other areas of government or the private sector, and tools or models that can be of practical use when designing and implementing strategies or initiatives.

Are you aware of research or other material that may directly or indirectly be relevant to the project? (If yes: please provide references).

Final remarks

Please feel free to include any comments or observations that you may have.

Part 2. Examples of implemented or planned initiatives

This template is designed to collect examples of how revenue bodies engage and involve SME taxpayers and stakeholders in order to improve compliance and achieve other benefits. The information collected will help build a picture of existing experience, emerging directions and important issues. This will in turn inform the project workshop and feed into the information note to be prepared to the benefit of all FTA members as well as other users of our products. We therefore kindly ask you to be as comprehensive as possible.

Please use a separate template for each example. You may of course provide as many examples as you like, but we encourage you to focus on two or three examples of initiatives where engaging and involving taxpayers contributed to significant results and valuable learning.

Name and contact details of respondent	
Name of initiative	
Background *What was the purpose and main elements of the initiative?*	
Nature and extent of engagement and involvement *Why (and how) was it decided to engage and involve taxpayers and stakeholders? What taxpayers and stakeholders did you engage and involve? What role did they have in the initiative? And how was this prepared and managed?*	
Results *What were the main results? And how did engaging and involving taxpayers and stakeholders contribute to this result?*	
Lessons learned *What are the most important lessons learned from engaging and involving taxpayers in this initiative?*	
Other perspectives and/or comments	

Thank you for your contribution!

Annex B. Additional resources

Below is a list of additional resources identified in the process of researching for this project. The list is intended as inspiration only and is by no means exhaustive. Mention does not imply endorsement.

Resource	Self description or other comprehensive summary
AccountAbility *www.accountability.org*	AccountAbility is a leading global organisation providing innovative solutions to the most critical challenges in corporate responsibility and sustainable development. Since 1995 we have been helping corporations, non-profits and governments embed ethical, environmental, social, and governance accountability into their organisational DNA. Our unique value proposition brings together leading-edge research, widely-recognised standards and strategic advisory services to deliver practical solutions for our clients.
Parciple *www.participle.net*	We believe there needs to be a new settlement between individuals, communities and government - new ways for people to get involved in determining their lives in a meaningful way, new approaches that mean some people do not get stuck at the bottom of the heap for generations and new bonds that mean people can flourish and bring their dreams alive. We also think that what matters is not just ideas, but real change on the ground, in our communities. On an everyday level this means public service reform - this is where the opportunities lie, to build something different. Participle's vision is radical: public services which offer all citizens a fair chance to realise their potential. For citizens to have this chance, it is not enough for society to present them merely with opportunities. There must be a shared commitment to developing citizens' capabilities, so that all can acquire the skills necessary to seize and shape opportunities. At Participle, we do two things: Firstly, bring together the widespread community level ideas and creative activity, and mix it with world-leading experts in any given field; Secondly, drive forward thoughts and actions around developing a new social settlement which can deal with the big social issues of our time.
International Association for Public Participation (IAP2) *www.iap2.org*	IAP2 is an international association of members who seek to promote and improve the practice of public participation in relation to individuals, governments, institutions, and other entities that affect the public interest in nations throughout the world.
Involve *www.involve.org.uk*	Involve are experts in public participation. We believe passionately in a democracy where citizens are able to take and influence the decisions that affect their lives. Through both research and practice we seek to radically transform the relationship between citizens and their governments to better use the creativity, energy, knowledge, skills and resources of all.

People & Participation *www.peopleandparticipation.net/display/Involve/Home*	People & Participation is based on Involve's successful book by the same name which was launched in 2005. The book provides a useful summary of participatory methods and practice but given the number of methods and speed of the development of new methods it is impossible for a printed publication to stay accurate for long. The reason for transferring People & Participation to the web is to allow us to maintain more, and more up to date information about participation. It also allows use as the site user to add your knowledge and experience making the site a truly collaborative experience, something that a book simply cannot do.
Public Policy Forum *www.ppforum.ca*	The Public Policy Forum is an independent, not-for-profit organisation dedicated to improving the quality of government in Canada through enhanced dialogue among the public, private and voluntary sectors. At the Forum we believe that good government, robust public policy and strong democratic institutions depend on the contributions of all sectors of society.
Australian Centre for Social Innovation *www.tacsi.org.au*	The Australian Centre for Social Innovation (TACSI) is a new kind of entity. We're not an academic institution, a service delivery organisation, or a government agency. We work in locally to lead large scale social change across Australia. We exist to identify and support the innovative ideas, methods and people that will contribute to and accelerate positive social change. Our ambition is to see more people lead thriving lives. We are a social innovation laboratory which creates, tests and incubates ideas, methods and projects for addressing unmet social needs and helping more people lead thriving lives. We are committed to finding, creating and sharing better methods for innovation in the social sphere. A key part of our mission is to bring together all sectors of society to find ways for it to be more resourceful, adaptive and resilient in tackling the big economic, social, environmental and cultural challenges of this century. This involves brokering relationships across public and private sectors, reaching across traditional boundaries between policy makers, social services, business and the community. To achieve our mission, we work with stakeholders including federal, state and local governments, businesses and non-government agencies.
Local Authorities Research Council Initiative (LARCI) *www.larci.org.uk* *www.rcuk.ac.uk/research/xrcprogrammes/OtherProgs/larci/Pages/home.aspx*	The Local Authorities Research Council Initiative (LARCI) established in 1997 to bring Local Authorities and the Research Councils into closer partnership has now reached the end of its funding. To replace LARCI the wide variety of research and knowledge exchange schemes that Research Councils run will be open to Local Authorities. This will provide new opportunities and encourage further and broader engagement between the Research Councils and Local Authorities.

Nesta.uk *www.nesta.org.uk*	Nesta is an independent charity with a mission to help people and organisations bring great ideas to life. We do this by providing investments and grants and mobilising research, networks and skills. Nesta doesn't work alone. We rely on the strength of the partnerships we form with other innovators, community organisations, educators and investors too. We're in the very lucky position of gaining greater independence and freedom at a time when many organisations face severe constraints. We hope that we can work with you to help bring your idea to life.
MindLab *www.mind-lab.dk*	MindLab is a cross-ministerial innovation unit which involves citizens and businesses in creating new solutions for society. We are also a physical space – a neutral zone for inspiring creativity, innovation and collaboration. We work with the civil servants in our three parent ministries: the Ministry of Business and Growth, the Ministry of Children and Education and the Ministry of Employment. These three ministries cover broad policy areas that affect the daily lives of virtually all Danes. Entrepreneurship, climate change, digital self-service, citizen's rights, emplyment services and workplace safety are some of the areas they address. MindLab is instrumental in helping the ministry's key decision-makers and employees view their efforts from the outside-in, to see them from a citizen's perspective. We use this approach as a platform for co-creating better ideas.
OECD Observatory on Public Sector Reform *www.oecd.org/document/57/0,3746,en_2649_37405_49086969_1_1_1_37405,00.html*	The OECD is developing an Observatory of Public Sector Innovation. The Observatory aims to systematically collect, categorise, analyse and share innovative practices from across the public sector, via an online interactive database. Today, the public sector in many countries faces the dual challenge of tight fiscal constraints, alongside more diverse and increasing demands on public services. The Observatory responds to these challenges by helping countries achieve the potential that innovation offers in improving public sector performance and delivering better outcomes. Innovation's role in fostering efficiency and effectiveness in the public sector was at the heart of the Public Governance Ministerial Meeting, held in Venice, 2010. Countries are already introducing innovative practices to their public services to differing degrees. However the conceptual understanding of what innovation means for the public sector, and what its impacts are remains limited. The Observatory aims to address these knowledge gaps by collecting, categorising, analysing and sharing country practices to create a common definition of public sector innovation, and to produce analysis so that countries can understand the benefits innovation can provide, and the factors which are important to its success.
Public Participation in Europe *www.partizipation.at/index.php?english*	

Annex C. Main enablers and barriers identified

Main enablers and barriers identified through survey and workshop discussions.

Enablers	Barriers
Committed and courageous leadership	Performance management regimes focusing on outputs rather than outcomes
Commitment expressed in government policies, revenue body visions or high level strategy documents	Challenges in establishing firm business cases for initiatives and documenting outcomes
Frameworks, tools and guidance	Expectations for quick wins and limited willingness (or ability) to invest in the medium or long term
Staff with specialist skills that can function as innovation ambassadors	Challenges and costs involved in changing legislation, systems and processes
Engaged staff willing to experiment and learn	More systematic and far-reaching forms of E&I often conflict with dominant culture and practices and provoke resistance
Training in creative processes, qualitative methodologies and user-involvement	Tendency to reach for solutions before problem is fully understood
Existing platforms (whether formal or informal) for consultation and collaboration with taxpayers and stakeholders	Risk aversion both internally among staff and management and externally among political stakeholders and external audit bodies
Increasingly obvious need for radical innovation to manage rising complexity, volumes and expectations	Overly formal approach to consultation
Opportunities offered by new technologies	Challenges in approaching and motivating SMEs and stakeholders, ensuring representativeness, managing expectations, and driving E&I processes to a successful end
Political demand for cost reductions and/or improved performance	Limited access to E&I specialist skills and training funds, and lack of frameworks, tools and guidance to support innovative practices
Shared interests with taxpayers and stakeholders	
Mutual trust between revenue body, taxpayers and stakeholders	

ORGANISATION FOR ECONOMIC CO-OPERATION AND DEVELOPMENT

The OECD is a unique forum where governments work together to address the economic, social and environmental challenges of globalisation. The OECD is also at the forefront of efforts to understand and to help governments respond to new developments and concerns, such as corporate governance, the information economy and the challenges of an ageing population. The Organisation provides a setting where governments can compare policy experiences, seek answers to common problems, identify good practice and work to co-ordinate domestic and international policies.

The OECD member countries are: Australia, Austria, Belgium, Canada, Chile, the Czech Republic, Denmark, Estonia, Finland, France, Germany, Greece, Hungary, Iceland, Ireland, Israel, Italy, Japan, Korea, Luxembourg, Mexico, the Netherlands, New Zealand, Norway, Poland, Portugal, the Slovak Republic, Slovenia, Spain, Sweden, Switzerland, Turkey, the United Kingdom and the United States. The European Union takes part in the work of the OECD.

OECD Publishing disseminates widely the results of the Organisation's statistics gathering and research on economic, social and environmental issues, as well as the conventions, guidelines and standards agreed by its members.

OECD PUBLISHING, 2, rue André-Pascal, 75775 PARIS CEDEX 16
(23 2013 19 1 P) ISBN 978-92-64-09651-6 – No. 60689 2013-01